Alexander Happy Christmas 1990.
With love from Mum and Dad.

A TEMPLAR BOOK

This 1990 edition published by Blitz Editions
An imprint of Bookmart Ltd
Registered No. 2372865
Trading as Bookmart Ltd, 60 Charles Street,
Leicester LE1 1FB

Devised and produced by Templar Publishing Ltd,
Pippbrook Mill, London Road, Dorking, Surrey RH4 1JE

Edited by Nicholas Bellenberg
Designed by Mike Jolley
Printed and bound in Yugoslavia by Grafoimpex

ISBN 1-85605-015-7

PICTURE CREDITS

Page 10: Sinclair Stammers/Science Photo Library. *Pages 10-11:* J.M. Start/Robert Harding Picture Library. *Page 11:* (inset) David Bayliss/RIDA Photo Library. *Pages 14-15:* Simon Conway Morris/Sidgwick Museum. *Pages 50-51:* G.S.F. Picture Library. *Page 51:* SUNAK-ZEFA. *Pages 58-59:* Ann Ronan Picture Library. *Page 72:* Mary Evans Picture Library. *Page 76:* Science Photo Library. *Page 80:* The Mansell Collection. *Page 105:* Mary Evans Picture Library. *Page 111:* Michael Lyster/London Zoo. *Page 116:* John Reader. *Pages 122-123:* Bernard Wood/ RIDA Picture Library. The Photo Source. *Page 129:* COMPIX. *Pages 130-131:* John Frost Historical Newspaper Service. The Mansell Collection. *Page 136-137:* ZEFA. *Page 140:* The Research House/NASA.

CREATURES OF THE PAST

Written by
JOHN STIDWORTHY
MA Cantab
Consultant Editor
STEVE PARKER
BSc Zoology
Illustrated by
CHRIS FORSEY

Blitz Editions

FIRST LIFE | PALEOZOIC

4·5 billion | 600 million | 225 milli

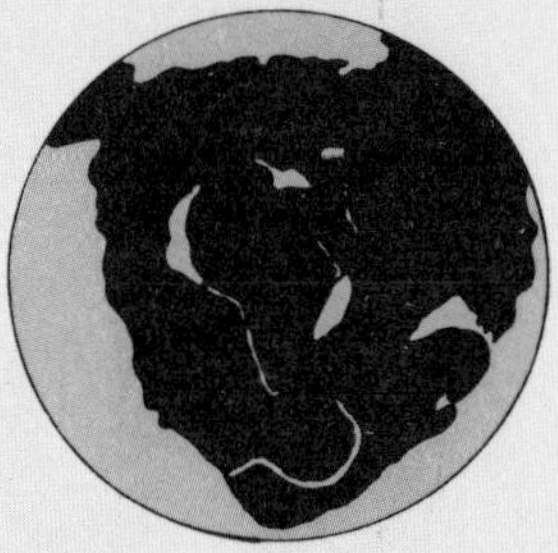

PART ONE

LIFE BEGINS

PART TWO

THE DAY OF THE DINOSAURS

MESOZOIC | CENOZOIC

65 million | Today

PART THREE

MIGHTY MAMMALS OF THE PAST

PART FOUR

THE HUMAN APE?

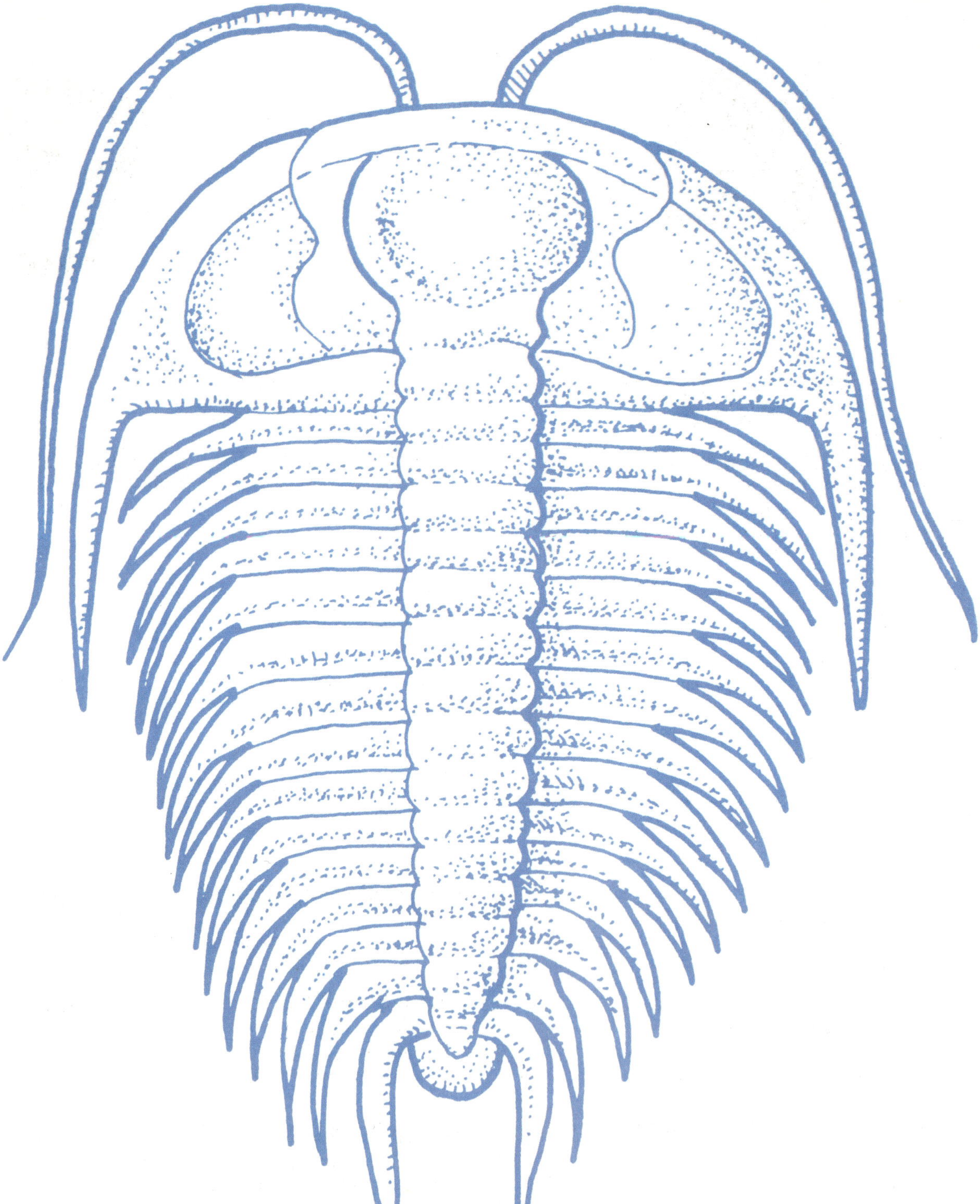

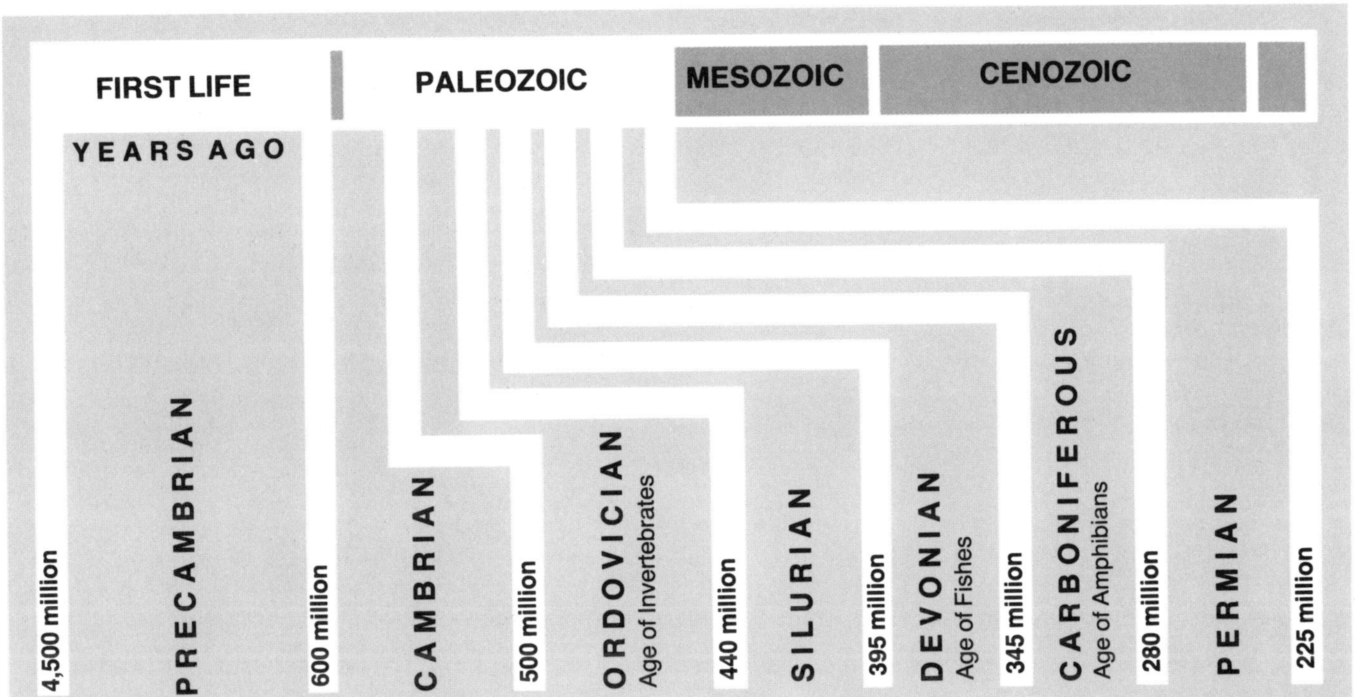

PART ONE

LIFE BEGINS

The origins of life on Earth are almost as much of a mystery as the beginnings of the planet itself. But in relatively recent years scientists have been able to piece together all the various discoveries, theories and clues to build up a picture of the past – of the Earth as it was 4,500 million years ago, right up to the present day. This, then, is the first chapter in the story of our planet and all those strange and wonderful creatures that once lived here . . .

THE DAWN OF TIME

The universe is vast beyond imagination. Planet Earth seems big to us, but it is quite small compared to some of the other eight planets that circle the Sun – our own star. The Sun is only one of the 100,000 million or so stars in the Milky Way – our galaxy. And the Milky Way is only one of the 100 million or so galaxies that we know exist in the universe.

All the galaxies are flying away from each other through space, like debris from an explosion. So it is likely that at some time they were all together in one place and that there was a 'big bang', which scattered all the matter in the universe. Scientists have calculated that this happened about 15,000 million years ago, and, in a sense, this was the beginning of time.

After the bang, some of the matter began to collect under the force of gravity, forming clouds of gas which became the galaxies. This process continued in each galaxy, gradually forming the stars. Debris from around the stars, in turn, came together to create planets.

About 6,000 million years ago, our Earth began to form when gases, dust, pieces of rock and metal came together under gravity. These melted and then the lighter rocks near the surface gradually cooled and became solid, forming the Earth's crust.

The age of some rocks can be measured quite accurately, and the oldest found on Earth date from 3,800 million years ago. This, then, is the approximate age of our planet, the stage on which life was to appear...

The origin of life

For millions of years the early Earth was boiling hot, with giant volcanoes erupting and throwing rock, dust and gases into the air. Electric storms flashed across the jagged new mountains and, as the atmosphere gradually cooled, rain lashed down on the rocks in storms that lasted for thousands of years. Nothing could live upon our planet.

The air of the early Earth contained no oxygen, which all animals and plants need to breathe to stay alive. But there were other gases in the atmosphere given off by the volcanoes, including nitrogen, ammonia, methane, water vapour and perhaps carbon monoxide and carbon dioxide. Most of these gases are poisonous to living things, so even after hundreds of millions of years, the Earth was not a very likely place for living things to appear.

Gradually, though, chemicals such as sugars and amino acids – which are found in living things today – began to build up in the seas and lakes. Nowadays, any sugars and other *organic* substances (those found in living things) floating in the sea would not last for long. They would be changed by the action of oxygen, used by animals, or absorbed by plants. Of course on the early Earth there was little oxygen, and no animals or plants, so these organic substances accumulated in the warm water until they made an 'organic soup'.

The chemicals in the soup then began to combine and change each other, producing different and more complex substances. Eventually, one with a special property formed – it could make copies of itself, which is one of the abilities that all living things possess. The substance that can do this is a long, curly, spring-shaped molecule called deoxyribonucleic acid (usually shortened to DNA).

Sometimes the copying process went a little wrong – enough to make the 'copy' slightly different from the original. When this happened nature could begin to choose' between the different versions. Life and the process of evolution had begun.

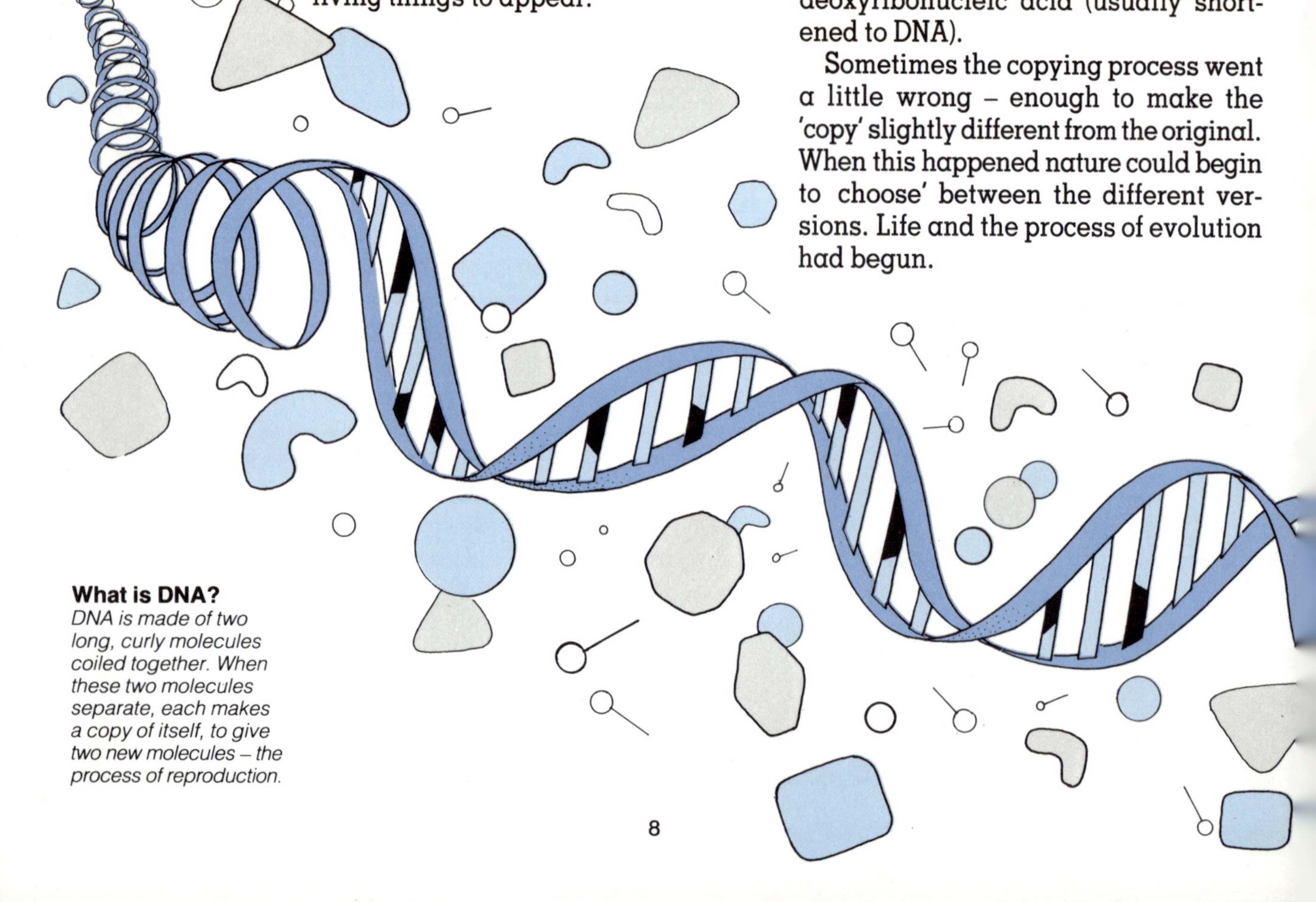

What is DNA?
DNA is made of two long, curly molecules coiled together. When these two molecules separate, each makes a copy of itself, to give two new molecules – the process of reproduction.

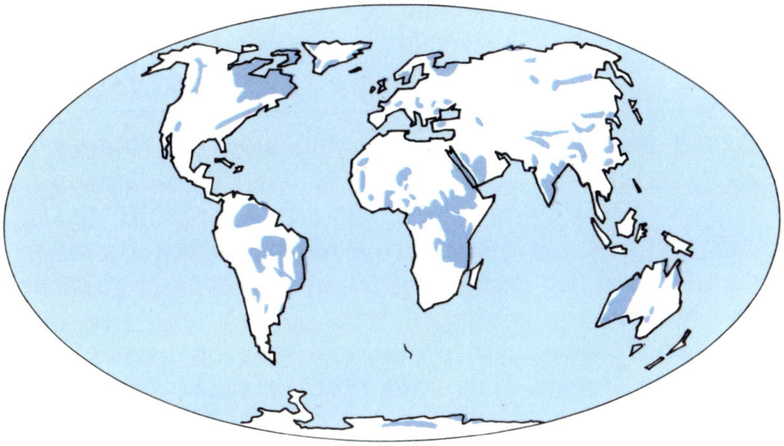

= Precambrian rock formations, about 3,800 million years old.

How old are the rocks?

The age of the Earth's oldest rocks, from around the time when life began, in the Precambrian period, can actually be calculated. Some rocks contain small amounts of substances that are 'radioactive', such as uranium 238. Over a period of time, this becomes less radioactive and changes to lead. (You can read more about this on page 18.)

It is a slow process – it takes 4,500 million years for half the uranium 238 in a rock to change into lead. Knowing this, scientists can carefully measure the amount of lead compared to the amount of uranium in a rock, and then work out how long ago it was formed. The oldest rocks on Earth have been found in Scotland, Canada, Africa and Australia. They are about 3,800 million years old.

The spark of life

In 1953 an American scientist called Stanley Miller filled a laboratory flask with a mixture of gases, like the ones that made up the atmosphere of the early Earth. He then fired large electrical sparks through them, just like the lightning bolts of early Earth storms. After a week of this, he found that a variety of substances had formed in the flask, including the amino acids and sugars that make up living things.

The first fossils

Fossils are the remains of plants and animals that have turned to stone. Until quite recently, it was believed that the oldest fossils were in rocks formed about 600 million years ago. But now we know that life goes back at least 3,000 million years, to the time we call the Precambrian, when the Earth was young. In fact, there have been living things for most of the time that our planet has existed. Scientists examining very old rocks have discovered the earliest signs of life – fossils preserved against all the odds for thousands of millions of years.

The first clue was the finding of *stromatolites* in the rocks. Stromatolites are rings, one inside the other, up to a metre across within the rock. Scientists wondered if they were made by a living creature, rather than simply being an odd formation in the rock.

Stromatolites in rocks from Lake Superior, in Canada, were the first to be thoroughly examined. Using special

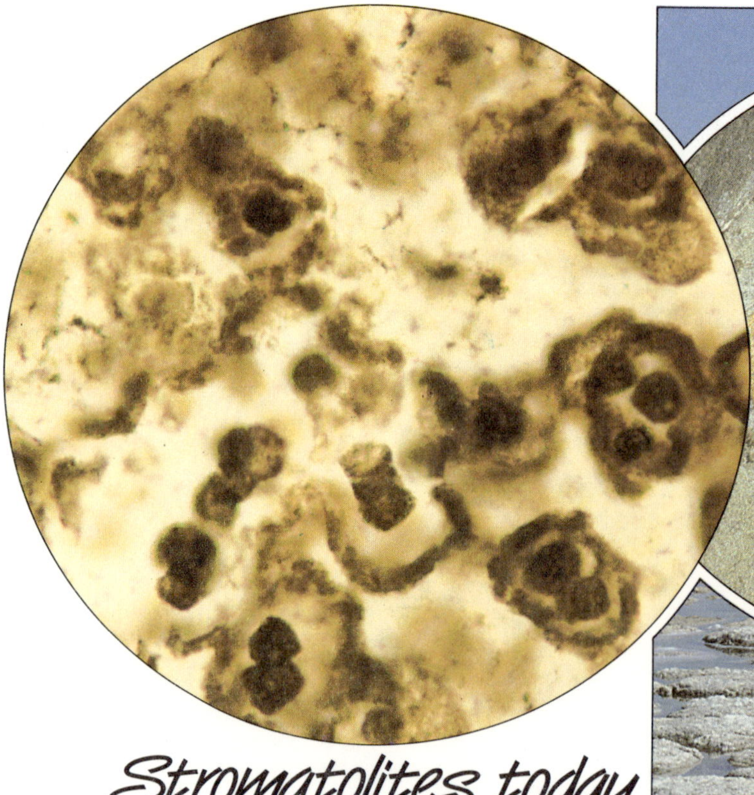

Stromatolites today

Stromatolites can be seen growing today in a few special areas, such as lagoons in Australia's Great Barrier Reef (picture, right). Blue-green algae extract the chemical lime, which is dissolved in the water, and turn it into solid stone columns. Slices of these columns, like that in the right-hand circle above, show the stromatolite-like rings seen in the oldest rocks. The left-hand circle above shows a highly magnified slice through a fossil stromatolite. You can make out the shapes of bacteria and algae – the oldest fossils known.

saws, scientists cut slices of the stromatolite-containing rock (a flint called chert), and then ground them so thin that light could shine through them. They could then be looked at through a microscope. The great surprise was that traces of living things could be seen – mostly outlines of what seemed to be cell walls. It was possible to see bacteria, primitive plant-like growths known as blue-green algae, and other remains less easy to recognize. So it appeared that stromatolites were indeed made by living things – they were in fact the first fossils.

The first cherts investigated were 'only' 1,900 million years old. Soon other rocks, 3,000 million years old, were studied and they contained these 'microfossils' too. Even older stromatolites are known from Australia, showing that blue-green algae were alive before this time. And some chert 3,800 million years old, from Greenland, has mysterious microscopic spheres inside it. These, too, could be the remains of some form of life – in which case they are the oldest fossils on our planet!

Small and simple

Blue-green algae (below) and bacteria (bottom) still thrive today and are the simplest living things. Each one is a single cell. It is made up of a skin or membrane surrounding a watery 'soup' which contains all the molecules the cell needs to live, grow, feed and reproduce. It has no complicated internal parts like a nucleus, which plant and animal cells contain.

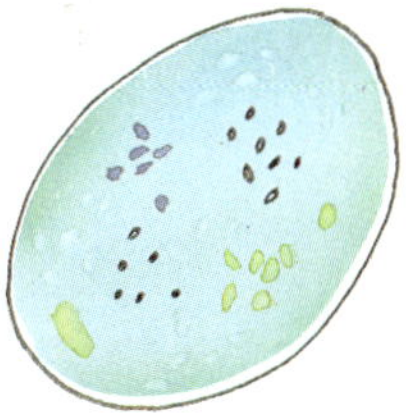

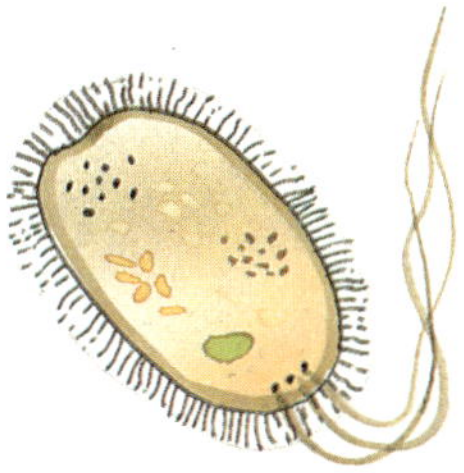

THE PRIMEVAL OCEANS

We can imagine what the teeming life in the primeval oceans was like, because of some extraordinary remains discovered in the rocks of the Ediacara hills, in southern Australia.

Today these rocks are hard sandstones, but 650 million years ago they were a soft, sandy beach on the edge of a sea. The dead bodies of sea creatures were washed up on to the beach and baked by the hot sun. Then, as the tide came in, they were buried by more sand. Their fossilized shapes survived as the sand was buried deeper and deeper and compressed into hard sandstone. Earth movements have tilted these rocks, wind and water have worn them away, and now the fossils lie on the surface.

All the creatures found at Ediacara were soft-bodied – that means they had no shells or bones or other hard parts. Their preservation in the fine-grained sandstone is almost a miracle for such soft creatures in such old rocks (you can read more about this on the next page). Although they are small, simple creatures compared to modern animals, they are much more complicated than earlier fossils. Many millions of years of evolution had to take place before animal life developed from the early bacteria to the jellyfish creatures of Ediacara. But we must wait until someone discovers fossils from the gap in between bacteria and jellyfish before we can know exactly what happened during this time.

How to say...

Spriggina
Sprig-een-a

Dickinsonia
Dick-in-sone-eea

Ediacara
Ed-ee-a-ka-ra

Foraminiferans
Fore-a-min-if-er-ans

Coccolith
Cock-o-lith

Ostracod
Ostra-kod

Jelly moulds!

It takes very special conditions for soft-bodied creatures to become fossilized. Usually, only animals with hard parts, such as bones, shells and teeth, are preserved as fossils. At Ediacara, which is shown on the previous page, there were special conditions. A beach with dead, sun-dried animals on it was quickly covered by fine sand. The finer the covering, the better the chance of small details being preserved.

Some of the finest fossils that scientists have ever found came from the Burgess Pass, in the Rocky Mountains of Canada. They were formed on the sea bed about 530 million years ago, in the middle of the geological period called the Cambrian. They are fossils of soft-bodied animals, and the special conditions allowed their jelly-like bodies to be moulded in solid rock.

All those years ago the area was probably a deep, calm valley on the sea bed. Towering above this submarine valley was an undersea mountain of soft, slippery silt. Sometimes there were massive avalanches on the mountain and a mixture of silt and water crashed into the valley below, engulfing some of the living creatures from above and burying them deeply. More and more silt piled up over the years, until eventually it hardened into solid rock, and the trapped animals were fossilized.

Because these animals were buried so quickly, perhaps in seconds, and by such fine silt, we can see incredible details in the fossils. Bristles, feathery gills, sometimes even muscles and intestines can be clearly seen. The conditions for preservation were so good that some of the animals found have never been seen anywhere else, before or since.

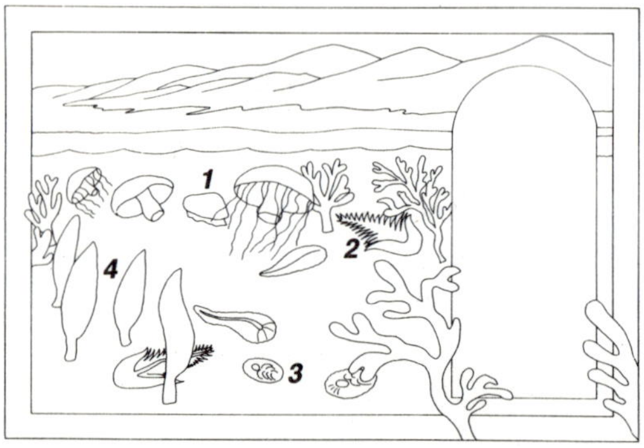

South Australia towards the end of the Precambrian

1 Jellyfishes *of many kinds pulsated through the seas. These 'underwater umbrellas' were much like the modern jellyfish.*

2 Spriggina *and other weird worms crawled along the bottom or swam with the help of paddle-like flaps on their bodies.*

3 Dickinsonia *was a rounded worm which may have wriggled along like a snake.*

4 Sea-pens *are coral-like animals, which form colonies shaped like old-fashioned quill pens stuck in the sea bed. Their fossils have been found in ancient rocks in central England as well as at Ediacara. Close relatives of these creatures still occur today.*

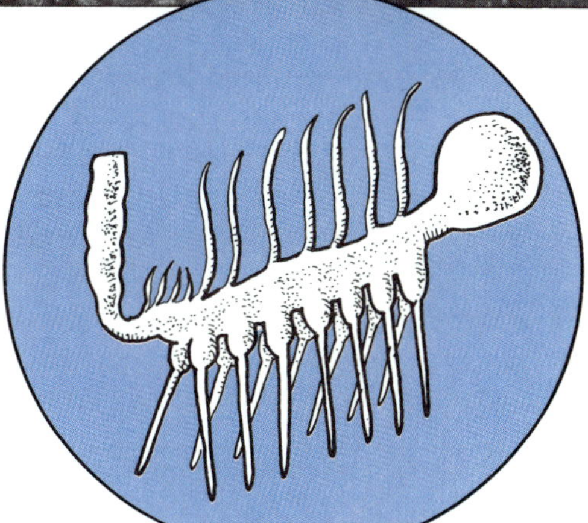

Can you believe it?

This strange creature was found among the Burgess Pass fossils. Called *Hallucigenia*, probably because the scientist who discovered it couldn't believe his eyes, it had seven pairs of legs, each pair with a tentacle above it. This animal is so odd that scientists have little idea to which present-day group it is related.

Common fossils

We tend to think of fossils as being rare finds. This is true for many groups, but there are some creatures and plants which were so common that whole layers of the Earth's rocks are made up of their remains. Three of these common groups are foraminiferans, coccoliths, and ostracods, shown below.

These and other "microfossils" in the rocks can be of great value to humans. Oil scientists know that particular microfossils occur in layers of rock which are often found above or below oil-bearing rocks. So the microfossils can be a helpful sign when test-drilling for new oilfields.

Foraminiferans

Foraminiferans are mostly microscopic single-celled animals, but they have hard shells with complicated patterns. Some limestone rocks are made up mainly of their skeletons. Foraminiferans are known from the Cambrian period onward.

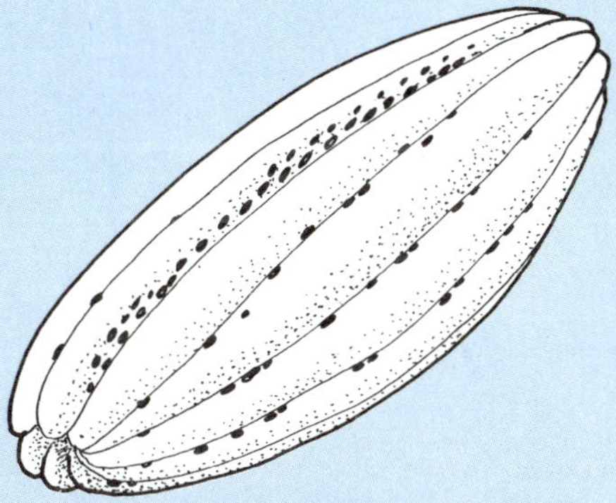

Coccoliths

The coccoliths are also "rock-makers." They are single-celled algae (plants) which have a shell made up of rings of lime crystals. When they die, the tiny rings fall to the bottom of the sea and gradually build up into limestone. They have helped to build many rocks, like the thick layers of chalk found in the Downs of southern England.

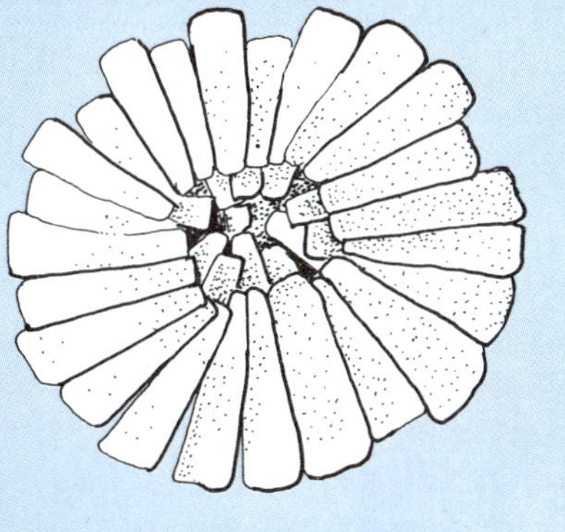

Ostracods

Ostracods appear in many rocks. These are relatives of shrimps, but look more like shellfish because their bodies are protected by a shell with two sides. Ostracods have been around for 450 million years. Most were tiny, but they were so numerous that when they died their tough little shells sank and made thick layers of rock on the sea bed.

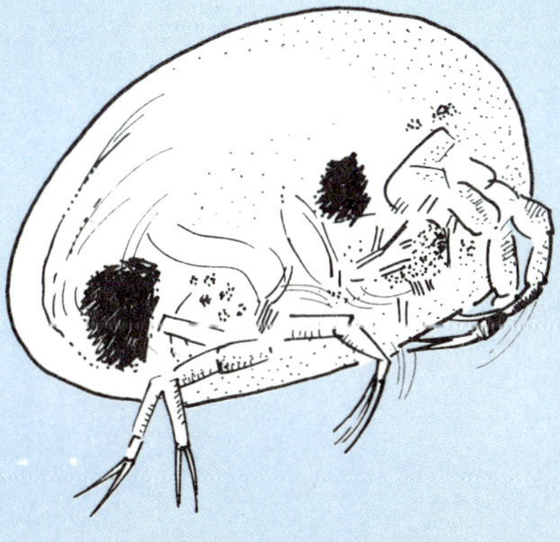

The time of the trilobites

One of the mysteries of life through the ages is when a successful group of animals, after flourishing for millions of years, becomes extinct. Scientists usually say that newer, more efficient animals evolved to replace them. But often it is not known why the newer group was better, or what was wrong with the old one! Sometimes we cannot even tell which animals *did* take over. A good example of such a mystery is the trilobite of the ancient seas.

The trilobites were one of the first big success stories of animal evolution. These creatures were divided into three along their length, a fact which gave them their name ('tri-lob-ite' meaning 'three-lobed'). Their bodies were made up of segments, and each segment had a pair of jointed legs, similar to shrimps' legs. At the front was a head with a pair of eyes on top, and at the back a tail.

Like crabs and insects, the trilobites had a hard outer body shell which gave protection to the softer parts inside. This skeleton was shed or moulted from time to time, so that the trilobite could grow. Many trilobite fossils are in fact fossils of these empty shells rather than of the whole animal. The fossils show the whole life-history of some species of trilobite, with up to 30 moults taking place between the tiny young larva and the fully-developed adult.

Many trilobites had legs around their mouths, which may have acted as 'jaws'. These would not have been very powerful though, so it is unlikely that they could catch and chew up large prey. Most probably they fed by scavenging on the sea bottom for small bits of plant and animal remains.

Trilobites were common in the Cambrian period (from 600 to 500 million years ago). They reached their greatest development shortly after, and then gradually declined. During their heyday at least 2,500 different kinds swam and crawled in the seas. But by about 225 million years ago all of them had become extinct.

Giant trilobite
Paradoxides *was one of the biggest trilobites, measuring 70 cms long. It lived about 550 million years ago.*

Seeing in the sea

Like its distant relatives, the insects, a trilobite had 'compound' eyes. This means each eye was made up of many individual flat sections, called *facets*, like a cut diamond. Each facet received light from only one direction. The whole eye then built up an overall picture of the surroundings by combining all the individual pictures from each facet.

The fossil trilobite on the right, a species of *Calymene* found in Czechoslovakian pyrite rock 500 million years old, has large prominent eyes. We can guess from this that trilobites must have lived mainly in shallow, calm seas. Deep water would not have been light enough to see in, and neither would stirred-up muddy water, so their eyes would have been useless.

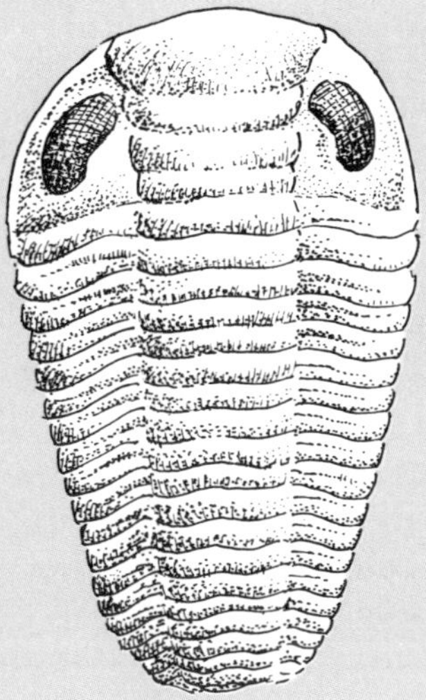

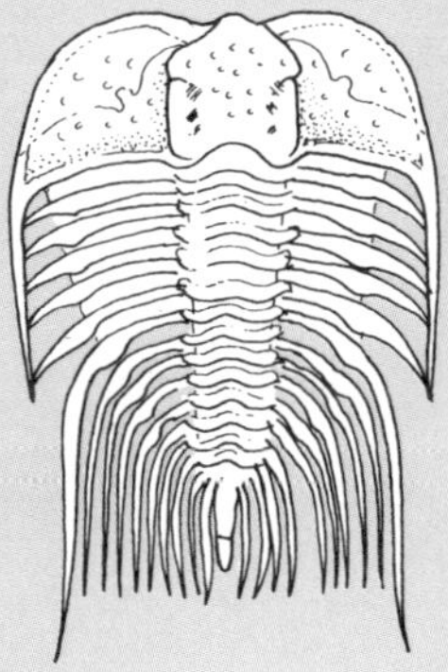

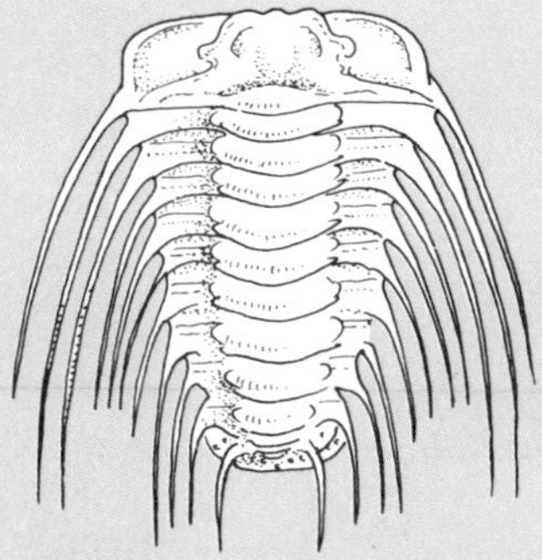

Smooth or spiny?

Two of the spiniest trilobites ever found are shown on the left. They are *Selenopeltis* (above) and *Cybeloides* (below) from the Ordovician period. Exactly why some trilobites had such long spikes all over them while others were quite smooth, is not clear. One theory is that the spines were useful for self-defence, since any predator trying to eat a spiny trilobite would get a prickly mouthful!

Trilobite armour

Smooth trilobites were protected against enemies by their tough skins, and perhaps some species burrowed into the soft sea bed so that they couldn't be turned over to expose their soft, vulnerable underparts. Others could curl up, like a woodlouse or hedgehog. One of these was *Calymene*. A lot of *Calymene* fossils have been found in a quarry at Dudley, near Birmingham. It was nicknamed the 'Dudley bug', and many remains show it curled up. They must have reacted to danger or bad conditions, then died in this position.

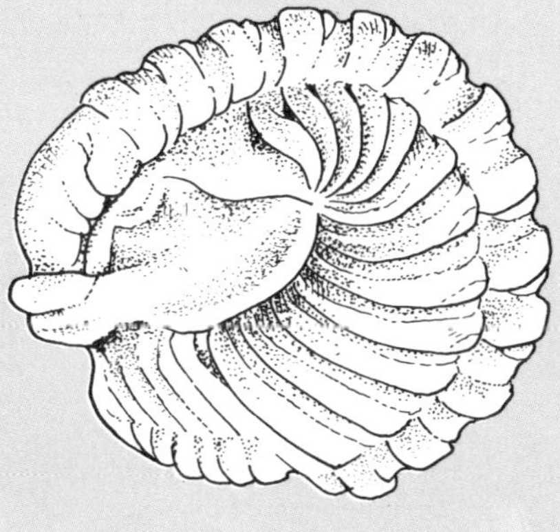

What became of the trilobites?

Trilobites seemed to be well adapted to their way of life, but died out as other animals evolved. We do not know the exact reason why, but they may have gradually been edged out by a whole range of competitors and predators.

The dating game

We know that the first living things appeared over 3,000 million years ago… We know that trilobites died out around 225 million years ago… But how do we *know* these dates? How can we tell when an animal or plant lived, just from its fossil?

In fact, there are various methods of *dating* a fossil – that is, using various clues to work out roughly how old it is. One method of detection is to look at the type of rock the fossil is embedded in, and at any other fossils preserved with it. Another way is to make measurements of what is called the *radioactivity* of the fossil or its rock, as explained on the right.

Because of the way fossils are made (pages 14, 81), they are usually found in sedimentary rocks. These rocks are formed in horizontal layers, one above the other, with the oldest layer at the bottom and the youngest at the top. It follows then that any fossils found in the lower layers must be older than those in the upper layers.

Looking closer, we find that each rock layer contains its own particular mixture of fossils. The mixtures change from

Dating indicators
Graptolites (top) and brachiopods (bottom right) are important 'index' fossils for dating. Graptolites are from the Ordovician and Silurian periods (500 to 395 million years ago). Brachiopods were very successful up to about 200 million years ago. The evolutionary changes in the distinctive shapes of these two creatures mean that they can be easily recognised and accurately dated.

Radiometric dating

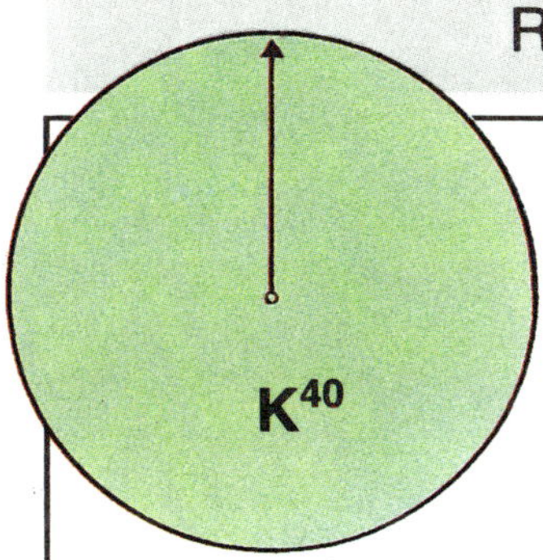

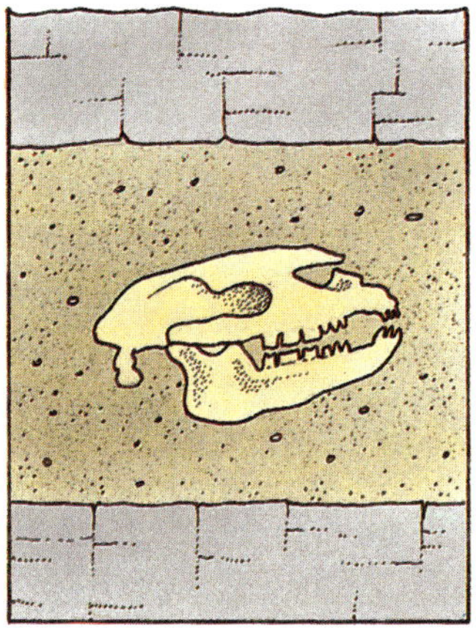

Ageing isotopes

1 Newly-formed volcanic rock that settles above or below sedimentary fossil-bearing rock contains something called an *isotope* of potassium. This is given the symbol K^{40} by scientists. As time passes the K^{40} decays into an isotope of argon, A^{40}.

2 The K^{40} decays into the A^{40} at a measurable rate. Half of the K^{40} will become A^{40} after 13,100 million years. This period of time is the isotope's *half-life*.

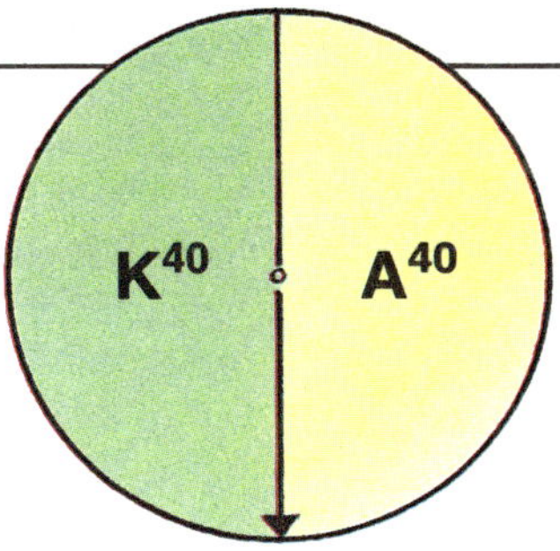

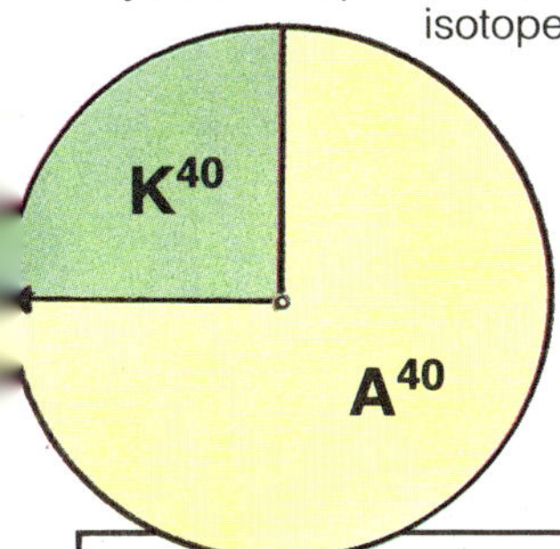

3 After another 13,100 million years, half the remaining K^{40} will become A^{40}.

4 When fossils are discovered, samples of volcanic rock from nearby can be analysed in a laboratory to work out how much A^{40} and K^{40} they contain. When the proportions of these isotopes are known, the age of the fossil can be deduced.

Other substances apart from potassium are also used in these *radiometric* measurements, and they all have different half-lives. Radiometric dating methods allow scientists to carry out *absolute* dating, and the results are very accurate.

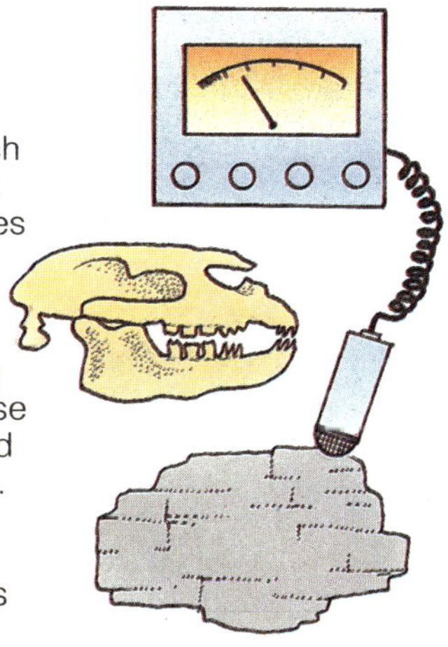

one layer to another because, as time passed, some animals became extinct while new ones evolved. The fossil mixtures also vary according to where in the world the rock layers formed, and whether it was a freshwater area or one covered in shallow seas or deep oceans. However, we have to be careful. The movements of the Earth's crust could have lifted layers, tilted them at crazy angles, or even turned them right over, and all this must be taken into account in the investigation.

The most useful fossils that make up the characteristic mixtures are of small, plentiful animals that had easily-preserved shells or other hard parts. Animals like this include molluscs (such as sea snails) and the ostracods and foraminiferans shown on page 15. Trilobites are helpful for the Cambrian period. Plant fossils are useful, too. Grains of pollen and seeds are plentiful and easily preserved and, like animal remains, they are found in characteristic mixtures which make extremely useful time markers.

So far, so good. We know how old one fossil is, relative to another. But can we give them real, *absolute* dates? The answer to this question is "Yes", and we do it partly by finding out how fast sedimentary rocks are formed today. Then, assuming that rocks were made at the same rate in the past, we can travel back in time by digging down into the Earth. If a fossil is buried a certain number of metres down, then we can work out roughly that it must have been trapped there so many millions of years ago.

But again, we have to be careful. Different types of sedimentary rock form at different speeds in different conditions. Also, we must remember that layers of rock which formed on top of the fossil may have been worn away in more recent times, giving us a false idea of how deep the remains really are.

THE SWARMING SEAS

In the Ordovician period, from 500 to 440 million years ago, the seas were filled with all manner of strange new animals. The first starfishes, sea-urchins and other echinoderms (spiny-skins) evolved. Early corals, helped by bryozoans (sea mats), built limestone reefs in the warm, shallow waters. These tiny animals lived together in colonies, each making a hard limestone skeleton.

The colonies varied greatly in size and shape between species. Some were flattened, others were upright, some were rounded and lumpy while others were thin and branching. The shapes of these animals and their reefs give us valuable evidence when dating the less common fish and other creatures preserved with them.

Other creatures, which had already evolved before this time, increased their success. The trilobites were at their most numerous. There were all shapes and sizes of brachiopods, which are also called lamp shells. The nautiloids, early relatives of the octopus, reached their greatest size. And water-living eurypterids, or sea-scorpions, stalked the sea bed and preyed on other animals.

This was truly the Age of Invertebrates, for almost all these animals, big and small, lacked backbones. But a new group of animals was beginning to develop. Although they were small, rare and not yet very important, the first vertebrates (animals with backbones) had evolved. Soon things on the Earth would change for ever.

How to say...

Lyssacina
Liss-a-seen-a

Chenendopora
Chen-en-dough-pore-a

Marrolithus
Marrow-lith-us

Opipeuter
Owe-pee-pewt-er

Scyphocrinites
Sky-foe-krin-eye-tees

Cheirocrinus
Keer-owe-krin-us

Eurypterus
Ewe-rip-tear-us

Giants of the ancient deep

The biggest animals of the Ordovician seas, some 450 million years ago, were the nautiloids. Some of these molluscs grew to over 4 metres long, with a straight shell narrowing to a point at one end and the creature's head at the other. In fact, a nautiloid looked rather like an octopus stuck in a multi-coloured ice-cream cone!

Nautiloids belong to the mollusc family. Molluscs are invertebrates (which means they don't have backbones), usually characterised by their shells. However, there are exceptions – like today's squids and octopuses, which don't have shells, but are still molluscs!

The nautiloid had lots of tentacles around its mouth, all-seeing eyes and was one of the swiftest sea-dwellers of its time. Not all were large, but still they must have been fearsome predators. Nautiloids were very numerous for a while, but by about 380 million years ago they were beginning to die out. Only six species remain today, the relatives of octopuses, squids and cuttlefish.

Sea-scorpions were another group of giant predators, but are not very well named. For a start, not all of them lived in the sea – they did evolve in sea water but some moved to slightly salty or even fresh water. They weren't true scorpions either, although they did belong to the arachnids – the group that includes spiders and scorpions.

A typical sea-scorpion, or eurypterid, had a long flat body made of segments. Its head had two large eyes, with two smaller 'eye spots' between them, and underneath were its walking legs. In front of these were two strong pincers.

A eurypterid looks 'multi-purpose'. It could have swum, walked or burrowed

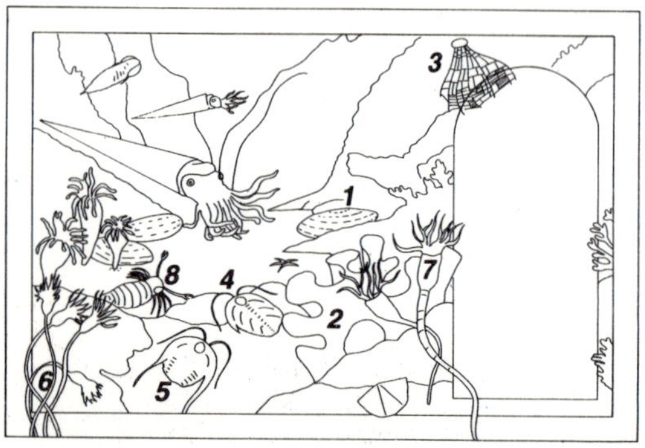

A shallow sea during the Ordovician period

1 Lyssacina, *and* **2** Chenendopora, *were sponges – very simple animals made of cells with tiny spiky pieces of silica for a skeleton.*

3 Dictyonema *was a net-shaped graptolite (page 18) about 10 cms long.*

4 Marrolithus, *and* **5** Opipeuter, *were trilobites of the time, only a few centimetres long.*

6 Scyphocrinites *was a beautiful sea-lily – not a plant, but an echinoderm. Its tentacles swept the water for tiny plant and animal food.*

7 Cheirocrinus *was a cystoid, an extinct type of echinoderm. Its waving tentacles collected food and its hollow body was held to the sea bed by a stalk.*

8 Eurypterus *was a sea-scorpion.*

Nautiloid in hiding
Orthoceras *lived about 410 million years ago. It could retreat into its shell and close it with a hard 'door' when danger threatened. It was about 1 metre long.*

in mud. But its main advantage was its size. Even the smaller sea-scorpions were large compared to the creatures they hunted, while the largest grew to nearly 3 metres long! Lying in wait near the sea bed, and grabbing prey when it came near enough, they were the tigers of the ocean before they finally became extinct.

Feeling the pinch!
Pterygotus *hunted in the seas about 400 million years ago. Its body was 2 metres long. Few animals (like the fish above) could have escaped from its terrible pincers.*

Tentacles, stars and spines

Many creatures, apart from those on the previous pages, became common then died out during the Age of Invertebrates.

Most of these animals had soft, fleshy bodies and no skeletons. Usually only hard parts like shells are preserved as fossils, but sometimes we are lucky. Some beautifully preserved belemnite fossils have been discovered in Bavaria, Germany. These show all the soft parts of the animal in great detail, and were formed by the same sort of 'lucky accident' that made the fossils of Ediacara and Burgess Pass.

Even if only fossil shells are found, palaeontologists can deduce what the rest of the animal looked like, by comparing the shell to that of a living relative. Fossil ammonite shells are very common, and very similar to the shell of *Nautilus*, a present-day nautiloid with a curved shell. Looking at the way *Nautilus's* body works, we can guess how ammonites might have moved.

In an empty *Nautilus* shell, you can see a line where a very thin part of the animal's body was partly embedded in the inside of the shell. The living *Nautilus* uses this part of its body to vary the amount of air that it keeps in its shell. If it pumps in more air, then the animal will be lighter in water and will rise nearer the surface. Absorbing some air from the shell will mean that the animal gets heavier in the water and will sink nearer to the bottom.

Fossil ammonite shells have a line in them, just like the *Nautilus* shell of today. This similarity means that an ammonite could probably rise and sink in a similar way to *Nautilus*. But we can only guess what the ammonites ate and what their soft parts looked like.

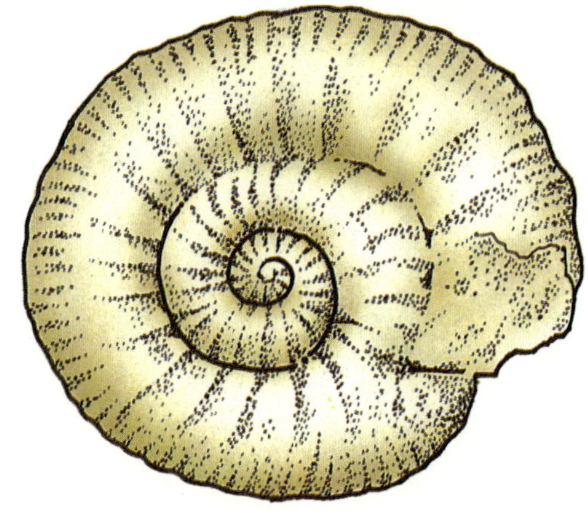

Fossil ammonite

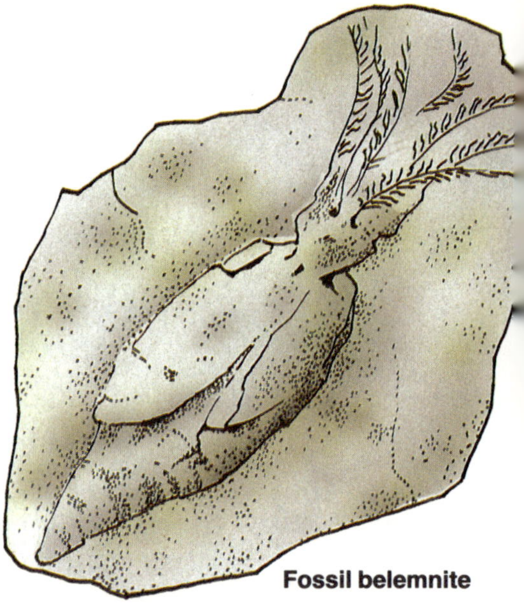

Fossil belemnite

Mollusc relatives

Ammonites and belemnites (living examples of which are shown on the right) were the relations of present-day molluscs – snails, squids and octopuses. They were common from 200 million to 65 million years ago. Ammonites evolved from the nautiloids and were very varied. Some were only the size of a coin, while others grew up to 2 metres across. They evolved very quickly, and are good dating 'labels'.

Belemnite fossils are usually of the creature's strong bullet-shaped shell. The whole creature was like a squid and probably swam backwards, trailing its tentacles behind it. The tentacles had rows of little hooks to catch prey, and inside its body the belemnite had an ink sac. It used to squirt out the ink to make a 'smoke screen' in the water when it was in danger – just like a modern squid does.

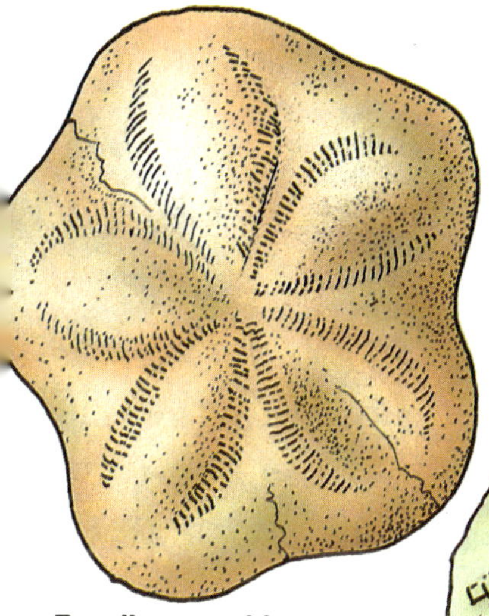

Fossil sea-urchin

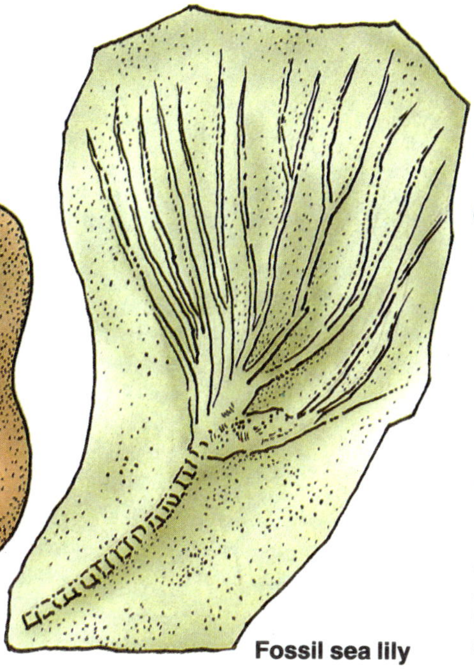

Fossil sea lily

Sea urchins and sea lilies

Sea-urchins and sea lilies (seen in their living form below) are members of the echinoderm group, dating from Ordovician times. Some sea-urchins are beautifully preserved as fossils, and early ones had thin shells made up of little plates like roof tiles. Both fossil and modern sea-urchins have tiny 'tube feet' which emerge from small holes in their shells. These feet are special to echinoderms. They are finger-shaped, fluid-filled bags, which can be pumped up and let down for walking, grasping and feeling.

Sea-lilies are not plants, but members of the crinoid family of echinoderms. They were actually known as fossils long before their living relatives were discovered in the depths of the oceans.

THE AGE OF FISHES

During the Devonian period, from 395 to 345 million years ago, there was an explosion in evolution. The first backboned animals, the fishes, appeared in enormous numbers and variety. They evolved first in the seas and soon made their way into freshwater rivers and lakes.

Many of the early vertebrates were not true fishes. They had backbones and they swam, but they had no jaws and lacked the paired fins found in real fishes. Even so, all the main groups of fishes living today began in the Devonian.

Things were beginning to happen on land, too. Several types of spore-bearing plants began to flourish there, such as horsetails, clubmosses and ferns. Some of these began to grow quite large, forming the first forests. With plants as a food source it was not long before the first land animals evolved. Insects were at the forefront of the land invasion, closely followed by the first amphibians (as you can read on page 33).

Meanwhile, back in the water the true jawed, finned fishes soon took over from the jawless versions. Some stayed small and insignificant; some evolved armour-plating to protect themselves from others who became the giant hunters of the Devonian deep, larger than the biggest sharks of today. Some, such as the placoderms, flourished briefly but quickly became extinct. By the end of the Devonian one group of fishes had moved on to yet another adventure – they had gained a finhold on the land!

How to say...

Dinichthys
Die-nik-thiss

Chirodipterus
Kye-row-dip-tur-us

Pteraspis
Tear-as-piss

Birkenia
Burk-een-ee-a

Lungmenshanaspis
Lung-men-shan-ass-piz

Climatius
Kly-mate-ee-us

Acanthodes
Ack-an-thow-dees

The first backbone?

One of the greatest advances in evolution was the development of the backbone. Fishes, amphibians, reptiles, birds and mammals – including humans of course – all have a backbone, or spine. When did this amazing feature evolve, and why was it so successful?

It is not known for certain which animal was the ancestor of the vertebrates (animals with backbones) but this is not really surprising. We are not sure what sort of creature we are looking for in the fossil record, or even whether it would have been fossilized at all since it might have been soft-bodied.

There is, however, one living creature that could tell us what the vertebrate ancestor may have looked like. This is a small eel-like animal called *Amphioxus*, otherwise known as the lancelet. It lives in the sea, usually with its body buried in sand and its head sticking out. It sucks water in through its mouth, filters out food particles, then pushes out the remaining water through its gill slits.

Instead of a backbone, this little creature has a pencil-like rod of strong tissue running down its back, called a notochord. Its main nerve cord runs just above. In vertebrates, the nerves are grouped together in a similar cord that runs up the spine to the creature's brain. So you can see why scientists believe that the notochord was the forerunner of the backbone. In fact, the young of backboned animals still pass through a stage with a notochord as they develop.

The importance of this rod (whether it's a notochord or a true backbone) is that it helps to stiffen and support the body, and it provides somewhere for the rows of muscles along the body to attach, so that they work efficiently. Animals like *Amphioxus* have been found in the Burgess shale rocks of 550 million years ago. This basic design for backboned animals has remained similar ever since, although the number of improvements has been enormous.

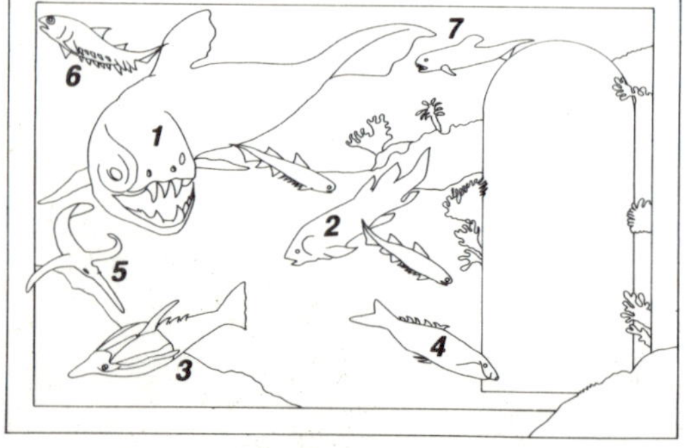

The warm waters of the Devonian

1 Dinichthys *was an arthrodire nearly 10 metres long. It was the largest animal of the time.*

2 Chirodipterus, *an early type of lungfish, looked similar to its relatives today.*

3 Pteraspis *(20 cms long), had no true fins and was probably a clumsy swimmer.*

4 Birkenia *belonged to the anaspids, which like the ostracoderms, had no jaws or true fins.*

5 Lungmenshanaspis *(25 cms in length) was a galeaspid, similar to an ostracoderm.*

6 Climatius *belonged to the acanthodians. Though shown here in the sea, it probably lived in fresh water.*

7 Acanthodes *was another acanthodian, one of the last survivors before the group died out around 260 million years ago.*

From gills to jaws

Gills allowed the next big leap forward in vertebrate design. Gills are the parts of a water-dwelling animal which absorb oxygen from the water, allowing the creature to 'breathe'. Gills were supported by bony bars in the first creatures to have them. But as evolution continued, the bars nearest the mouth changed their job and position, bending around the mouth to form an upper and lower jaw. The skin in this area grew bony scales which were much bigger and sharper than ordinary body scales. These developed to become teeth. The fish, as it had now become, was able to bite and chew larger lumps of food, and even catch large animals.

This was a great advance. Jaws meant that many more ways of life were possible, instead of just filter-feeding or sucking up tiny food particles from the sea bed. The fishes evolved rapidly to take advantage of these new evolutionary 'inventions' and soon the seas swarmed with jawed, finned vertebrates.

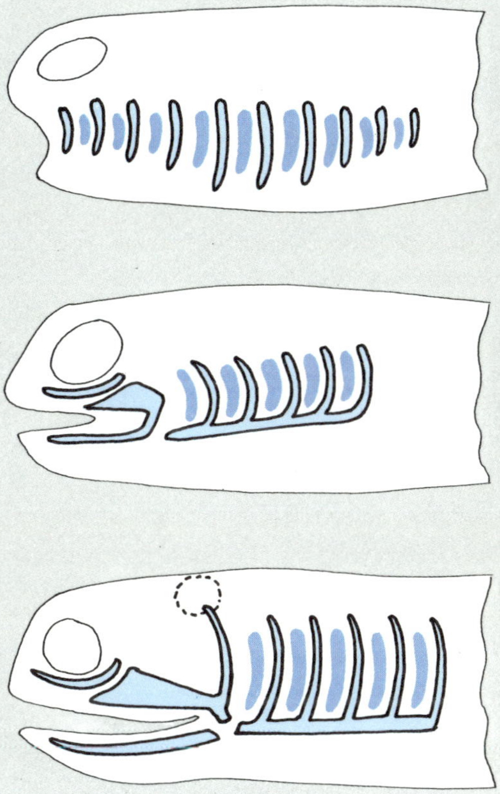

= Bones
= Gill slits

Useful gills
1 *In a primitive ostracoderm there is a row of gills, each one the same and supported by a bony bar.*

2 *In a more advanced fish, an acanthodian, the first gill bars have become bony plates in the eye socket. The second gill bars have bent forward to form the jaws.*

3 *In an even more advanced fish, a fossil shark, the third gill bars have become part of the hearing organ. What were the fourth gill bars are now the first!*

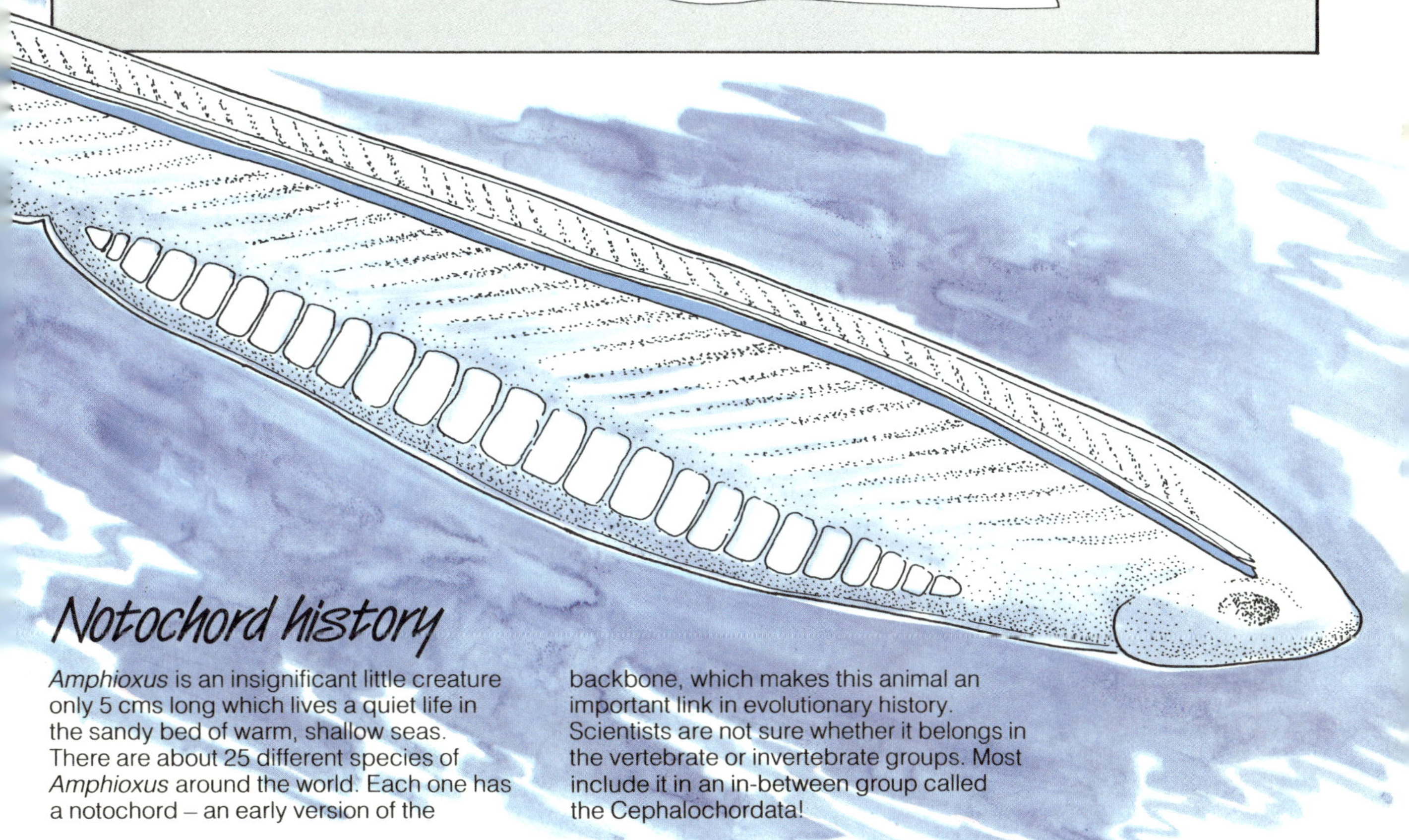

Notochord history

Amphioxus is an insignificant little creature only 5 cms long which lives a quiet life in the sandy bed of warm, shallow seas. There are about 25 different species of *Amphioxus* around the world. Each one has a notochord – an early version of the backbone, which makes this animal an important link in evolutionary history. Scientists are not sure whether it belongs in the vertebrate or invertebrate groups. Most include it in an in-between group called the Cephalochordata!

Spines and armour

As the Age of Fishes continued, various groups evolved and died out. The ostracoderms, anaspids, galeaspids and acanthodians (all mentioned on the previous pages) eventually disappeared. So did the placoderms, yet another group of armour-plated fish. But in the middle of the Devonian period, 370 million years ago, placoderms ruled the seas.

Some placoderms, like *Pterichthyodes*, were quite small. This type had a strange bony armour, which went not just over its head and body, but down its front fins too. Scientists believe that this fish crawled along the sea bed using its fins as stilts or 'legs', because some of the fossils show signs of wear on the ends of the fin covers.

The largest placoderms are called arthrodires. These had strong shields on their heads, hinged to equally strong plates on their chests. At the back end some species had scales, although later arthrodires had bare skin near the tail. *Coccosteus* is a well-known fossil arthrodire.

On fossil arthrodires of all shapes and sizes there are grooves in the armour plating, running along the body. These probably contained the sensitive 'lateral line' that fishes have today. It helps them 'feel' water currents and other animals' movements. So this useful feature evolved very early on in vertebrate history.

The arthrodires reached their peak late in the Devonian period, in terms of both numbers and size. In fact, some became bigger than any previous animal, and bigger than most fishes since. The biggest was the giant *Dinichthys* – nearly 10 metres long!

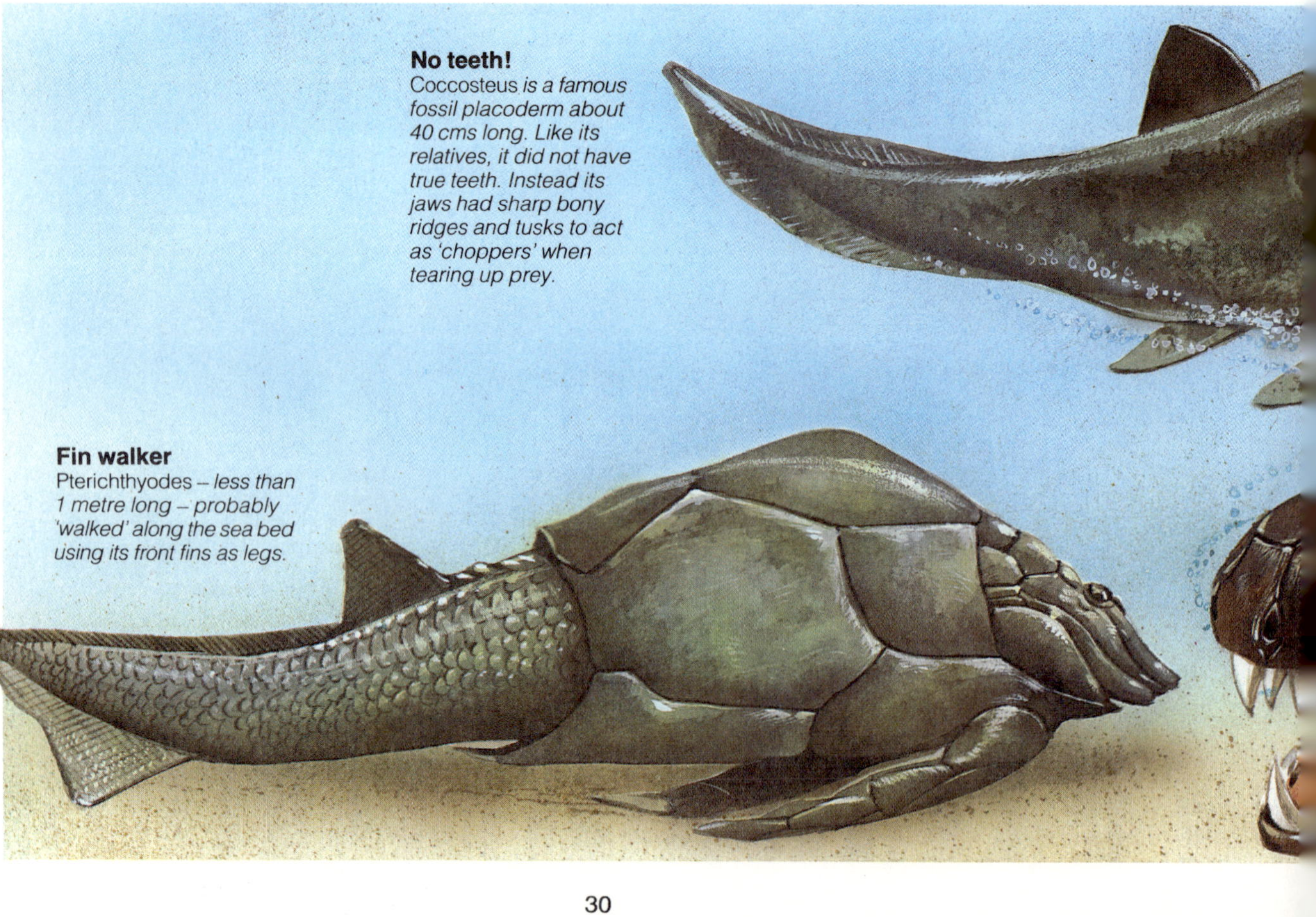

No teeth!
Coccosteus *is a famous fossil placoderm about 40 cms long. Like its relatives, it did not have true teeth. Instead its jaws had sharp bony ridges and tusks to act as 'choppers' when tearing up prey.*

Fin walker
Pterichthyodes – *less than 1 metre long – probably 'walked' along the sea bed using its front fins as legs.*

The successful shark

Sharks first appeared in the Devonian period. They are sometimes referred to as 'primitive' fish, but that does not mean they are inefficient or badly designed. It just means that they evolved a long time ago. Although their descendants have changed in some ways, the same overall design is as successful now as it was nearly 400 million years ago.

Sharks' skeletons are not made from bone, but cartilage, which is quite soft and unlikely to fossilize. Most fossil sharks are known from their preserved teeth, but occasionally some whole fossil sharks are found. One such is the streamlined *Cladoselache*, from the late Devonian, which was preserved in shale rock in America.

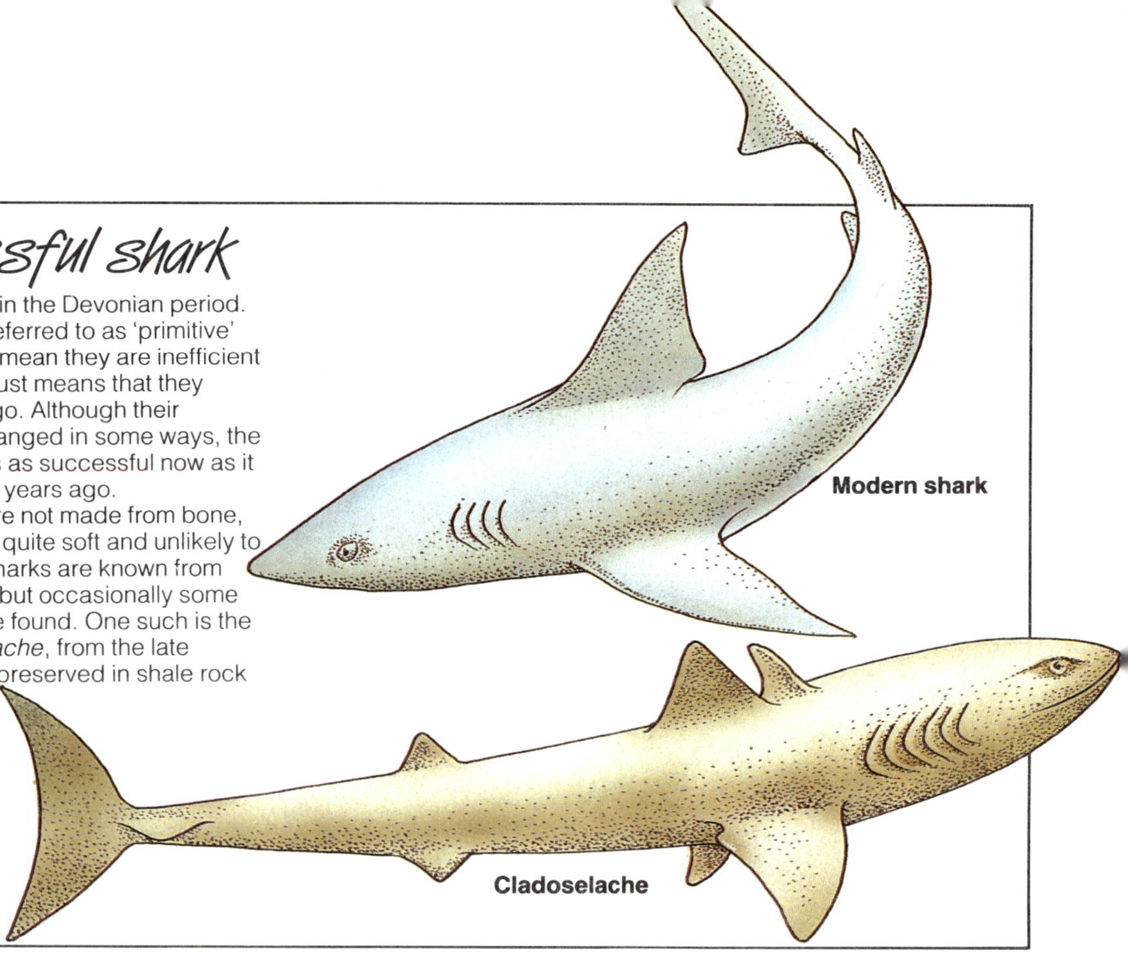

Bone blades
Dinichthys *was a fearsome giant of its time. Its huge mouth was armed with cutting blades of bone 60 cms high.*

THE AGE OF AMPHIBIANS

The Carboniferous period, from 345 to 280 million years ago, is often called the Age of the Amphibians. Although fishes flourished in the seas and many plants and insects lived on the land, amphibians were the most advanced animals of this time and evolved quickly. They lived on land *and* in water. They laid their eggs in the water; the eggs hatched into swimming tadpoles; and as the tadpoles became adult they moved on to the land.

Huge steamy, swampy forests covered large areas of the Carboniferous world. These swamps provided ideal habitats for amphibians. The 'trees' in these forests were actually giant horsetails and clubmosses, crawling with cockroaches, giant dragonflies, spiders and scorpions. So there was plenty of food for the amphibians as they crawled from the water.

Many early amphibians were shaped like their modern descendants, the newts – but some were 2 metres long, much larger than any amphibian alive today.

At the end of the Carboniferous, the Age of the Amphibians was nearly over. Many died out, a few stayed as they were, while others returned to the water full-time. The remainder were able to move permanently onto the land, because their eggs had developed shells and so they no longer needed to lay them in the water. So the amphibians became reptiles – the creatures which were soon to dominate the world for hundreds of millions of years.

How to say...

Dolichosoma
Doll-itch-oh-so-ma

Eogyrinus
Eee-oh-gee-rine-us

Meganeura
Meg-an-new-rah

Discosauriscus
Disco-saw-iss-cus

Calamites
Cal-am-ite-ees

Sigillaria
Sig-ill-air-ee-ah

Psaronius
Sar-own-ee-us

From fins to legs

By the end of the Devonian period the bony fishes had evolved into two main groups. One was the 'ray-fins'. These went on to become very successful. Nearly all the 20,000 bony fish species living today are ray-fins.

The second group was the 'lobe-fins'. About 300 million years ago they were very numerous and successful. Today there are only a few species left. But they 'live on' in another way, because their lobed fins gradually evolved into legs! All land animals with backbones – amphibians, reptiles, birds and mammals – are in fact descended from the primitive lobe-finned fish.

This evolutionary step may have happened because in the Devonian period, some parts of the world seem to have had a changeable climate. Lakes and ponds must have filled up and dried out quite regularly. A fish with lobe fins might have been able to push itself across a mud-bank to a bigger pool, to escape when its own pool dried up. The ray fin, being much weaker and more flimsy, probably could not do the job as well.

The lobe-fins had another advantage over the ray-fins. Inside a fish's body is a hollow bag called a swim bladder. This contains air, to make the fish lighter so that it can swim more easily. In most ray-fins the swim bladder is not connected to the mouth. But in a lobe-fin it *is* connected to the mouth, by a tube in the throat. So the lobe-fin can gulp air into its swim bladder. When a Devonian pool dried up, this could come in useful as a temporary way of breathing. In fact, there are still some fish alive today – the lungfish – that do exactly this. It was the first step in the change from fish to amphibian, and it took place in the Devonian. As one pool dried out, lobe-finned fish could crawl to another one on their strong fins, gulping air as they went. *Eusthenopteron* and *Ichthyostega* are two fossil creatures which show us how the change probably took place.

A 'living fossil' ?
Coelacanths were a group of lobe-fins which were common from 370 million to 70 million years ago. After that time, they disappeared. But one species of coelacanth was rediscovered in 1938, living in the depths of the Indian Ocean. However scientists do not believe that the modern coelacanth is a 'living fossil', similar to the ancient coelacanths.

Ancient coelacanth

Modern coelocenth

Life in a Carboniferous swamp

1 Dolichosoma *was an early amphibian, though it looked like a snake. (Snakes had not yet evolved.)*

2 Eogyrinus *(3 metres long) was another amphibian that looked like a reptile – in this case, a crocodile.*

3 *Giant insects such as the dragonfly* Meganeura *and early cockroaches crawled and flew among the Carboniferous plants.*

4 Discosauriscus *was an amphibian 40 cms long.*

5 Calamites *– giant horsetails – grew up to 20 metres tall.*

6 Sigillaria *was a giant clubmoss, 15 metres high.*

7 *The tree fern* Psaronius *grew up to 8 metres tall. It is the ancient relative of some of today's ferns.*

Skin and bones

In a ray-finned fish (below), each fin has a narrow base. The main part of the fin is supported by thin fan-shaped rays, which are made of hardened skin.

In a lobe-finned fish (bottom), there is a solid lobe of flesh at the bottom of the fin. The main part of the fin is supported by bones within this. Skin rays are just on the outer part of the fin.

Eusthenopteron (the fish at the bottom) was a lobe-fin about 1 metre long. The bones in the lobe part of its fin were arranged with one long bone nearest the body, then two bones next to it, and a collection of smaller bones towards the outside. You can see this in the left hand circle. The bones inside a limb have a similar arrangement, and are shown in the right hand circle.

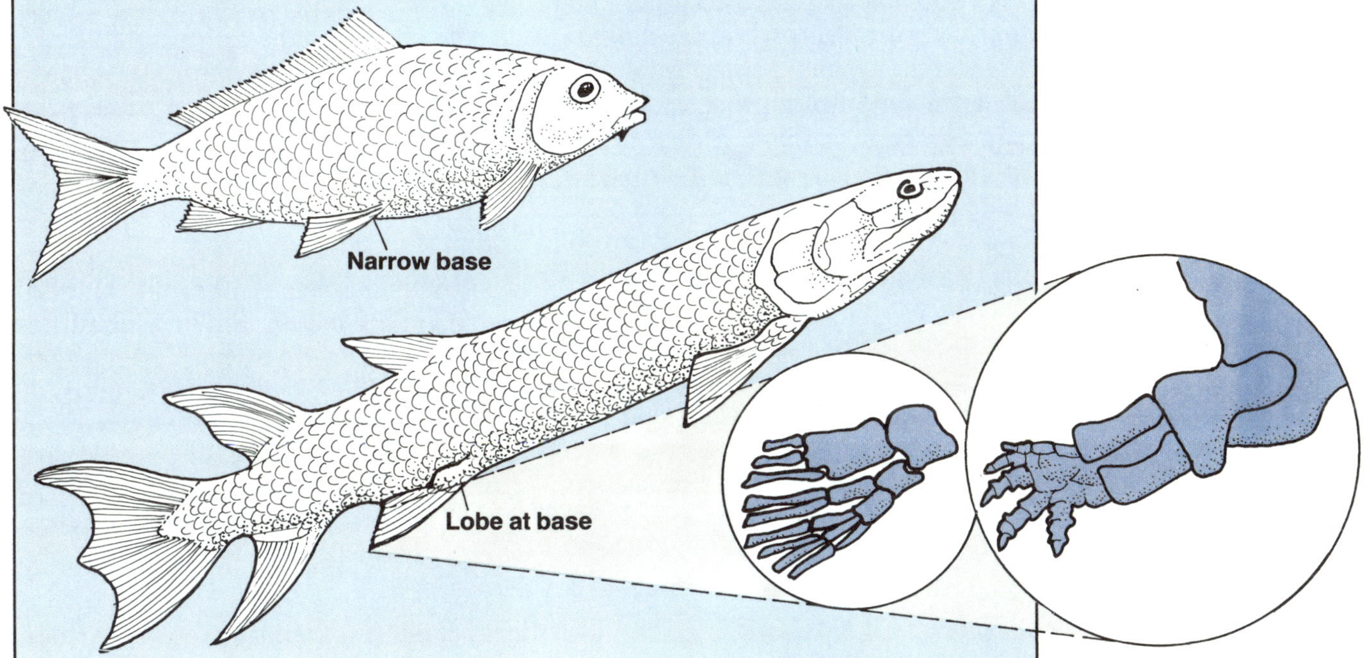

The first amphibian
Ichthyostega was the first amphibian. About 1 metre long, it still had a fin along the tail, but its other fins had turned into legs. Each foot had five fingers. The fossils of adults show no sign of gills.

The amphibians stride out

When the amphibians moved on to land, life was easier in some ways. Food was abundant, and there were few other large creatures to compete with. But there were plenty of problems to overcome.

Air does not support an animal's body as well as water. Legs, hips, shoulders and backbone needed strengthening to allow the amphibians to move easily in their new surroundings. *Eryops*, of about 260 million years ago, had strong legs and a powerful backbone to support its 2 metre long body on the land. But like other amphibians, its legs jutted out from the side of its body. This made it difficult to lift the body clear of the ground. (When the reptiles evolved, this was one of the problems they solved, by having their legs underneath their bodies.)

Living on land made seeing difficult, too. Fishes' eyes are constantly bathed in water and so are always clean and moist. In air, this sort of eye would dry up and get dirty. So eyelids evolved to protect the eyes – they were able to blink and wipe the surface of the eye clean. Special tear glands also developed to make tears which kept the eyes moist.

Hearing was another problem. Sounds travelling through water also travel through the body of a fish. So ears deep in the fish's body can register the sound. But on land things are much different. Many sounds travelling through the air would simply bounce off an amphibian's body. To hear, it needs ears on its body's surface. So two thin areas of skin, the eardrums, evolved on the surface just behind the head. A small bone which was part of the jaw support in fishes (see page 29) became attached to this, to conduct sounds to the deeper part of the ear.

Despite these and other adaptations, by about 200 million years ago the giant amphibians had faded out. Their representatives today are frogs, toads, newts, salamanders and a few burrowing, legless worm-like creatures called caecilians – small reminders of their huge relatives that once roamed the Earth.

Leather skin?
Eryops remains have been found mainly in America. Its skin was leathery, with only small scales and it probably fed in the water, catching smaller amphibians and fish.

The end of an era

Once the reptiles evolved and became established on land, they forced most large amphibians to die out or return to the water. Some 210 million years ago the huge flattened amphibian *Paracyclotosaurus*, which was over 2.5 metres long, remained in the water. There was also a group of small but very odd water-living amphibians, that had feeble legs and a head with flat bony 'horns' on each side. The last and oddest of these was *Diplocaulus* of about 260 million years ago, with a body about 60 cms long.

Diplocaulus

Paracyclotosaurus

Tadpole with a beard

The soft bodies of amphibian larvae – tadpoles – are preserved very rarely as fossils. This tadpole-like creature, *Gerrothorax*, from 210 million years ago was about 80 cms long. Like today's tadpoles it had feathery gills that it used for breathing in water.

Yet this wasn't a larva. *Gerrothorax* was a mature adult, able to breed. This odd mixture of a young, larva-type creature which can breed like a normal mature adult is called *neoteny*. It still occurs today in some amphibians, such as the axolotl.

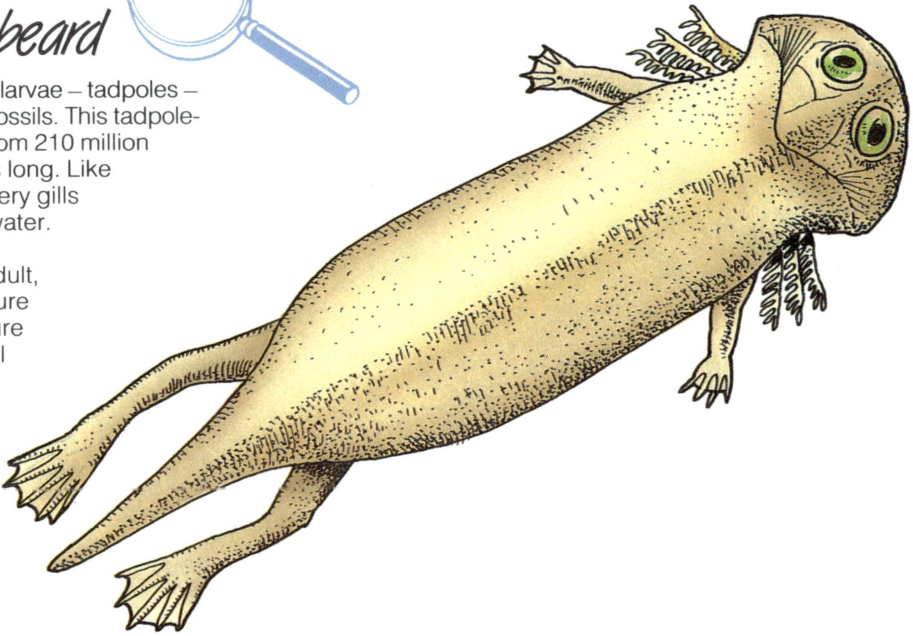

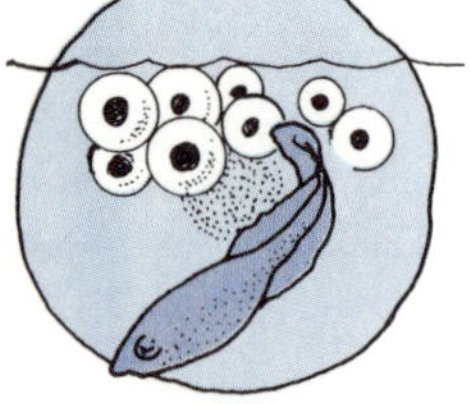

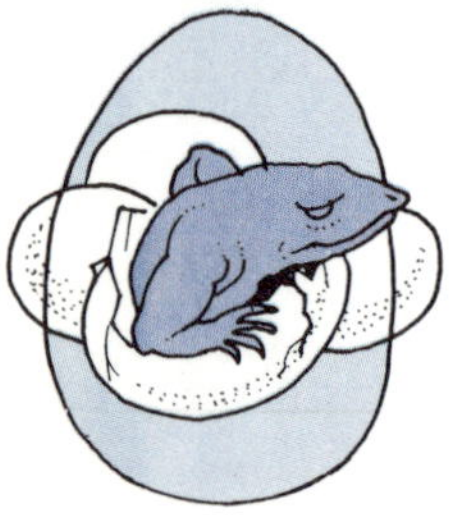

Soft or hard eggs?
The amphibian's egg had no shell. It had to be laid in water, where its young also lived. Both eggs and tadpoles were in great danger of being eaten.
The reptile's egg had a leathery or hard shell instead. It could be laid on dry land, hidden from predators.

The magic egg!

Although the Age of Amphibians lasted a long time – many tens of millions of years – the amphibians themselves could never leave the water behind. This was where they laid their eggs, and where their tadpoles grew up. Many adult amphibians had damp, slimy skins that needed to be kept moist by regular swims. They were mostly fish-eaters, and had the pointed teeth of their fishy ancestors. Even a late amphibian like *Eryops* still had the same type of teeth as the fish *Eusthenopteron*.

But some of the amphibians did evolve. They developed a waterproof skin so that they could move from damp areas to really dry places. And they evolved a waterproof egg that could be laid on land, in other words, they became reptiles.

Before the end of the Carboniferous period, 280 million years ago, the first reptiles had evolved from amphibians. We can work this out from fossil skeletons, even though the most important advances, the scaly skin and shelled egg, have not generally fossilized.

Besides the waterproof scaly skin and the shelled egg, early reptiles also found a new food source – land plants. These were much tougher than water plants, so the front teeth of some reptiles became chisel-shaped for cutting leaves, while the back teeth took on a flat shape for chewing.

Reptiles gradually took over from amphibians during the Permian and Triassic periods, up to 195 million years ago. From then on, dinosaurs and other giant reptiles ruled the world for millions of years. The Day of the Dinosaur had arrived...

Reptile or amphibian?

Seymouria lived about 260 million years ago. In almost every part of its body it was midway between an amphibian and a reptile. At one time it was thought to be the ancestor of all reptiles. Now scientists believe it was an amphibian with reptile-like features, on a side-branch of the main evolutionary tree.

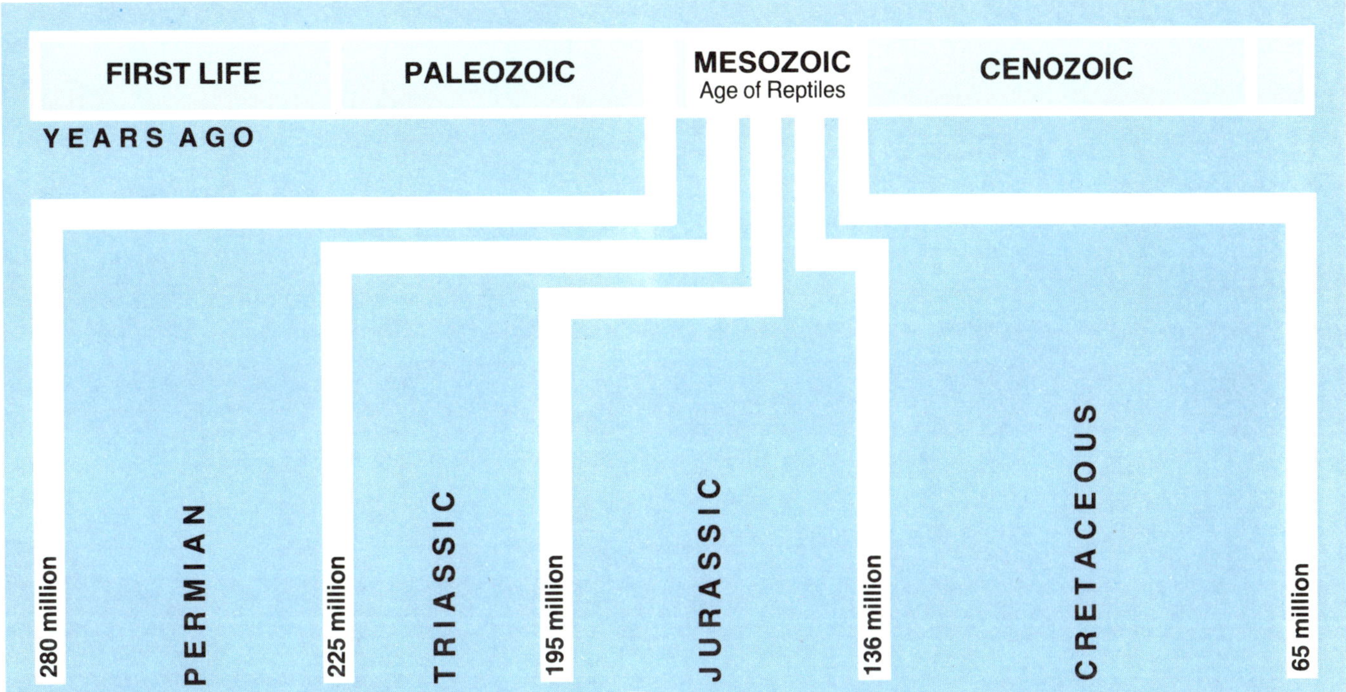

PART TWO

THE DAY OF THE DINOSAURS

Out of the great swamp regions of the Carboniferous period came the reptiles – the first backboned animals to ever live entirely on the land. They came to dominate the world as they evolved into a great diversity of species – from the huge plant-eating *Diplodocus* to the tiny, flying *Pterodactylus*. Perhaps the best known reptiles of this time were the dinosaurs who successfully ruled the planet for over 100 million years. Their story starts 280 million years ago, when the days of the dinosaur were just about to begin . . .

REPTILES RULE THE EARTH

During the Permian period, from 280 million to 225 million years ago, the reptiles gradually took over the world. The very first reptiles lived long before this time, but they were scarce animals in a world dominated by large amphibians.

By 280 million years ago the amphibians were becoming less common and the reptiles had evolved into many types and sizes, all with different ways of life. Some were small and lizard-like – though the true lizards came along later. Others were large and clumsy. Some were plant-eaters with tough, broad teeth that could crush the Permian vegetation. A few even evolved sails on their backs, which may have helped them to control their body temperature (see page 44).

The earliest reptiles probably lived partly in the water. As time went on they were able to leave the water completely and live on the land. Most of these new land-dwellers had heavy limbs which stuck out sideways from their bodies. They had solid skulls and small brains. They laid eggs with shells, that didn't have to hatch in water. They had mastered the basics of living on land, but they must have been clumsy and slow compared to the more advanced reptiles that came later.

As the reptiles prospered, the amphibians declined. By the end of the Permian the Age of Reptiles was well under way – a reign that was to last for another 160 million years.

How to say...

Araeoscelis
Air-ee-owe-skell-is

Captorhinus
Cap-tow-rine-us

Pareiasaurus
Par-rye-ah-sore-us

Edaphosaurus
Edd-aff-owe-sore-us

Dimetrodon
Di-met-trow-don

Leaving the water

As the Permian period passed, many new reptile species appeared and rapidly took the place of the amphibians. Yet many of these new reptiles looked very similar to the amphibians they were replacing. So what made them better?

The answer seems to be that their lives had become completely independent of the water. Several adaptations helped the reptiles to do this, like having a dry, scaly skin which does not let water escape from the body. Most amphibians have a smooth, slimy skin, which allows water to evaporate quite quickly. So amphibians had to stay near water or damp places, to keep their skins moist – otherwise they would dry out. Reptiles, on the other hand, could move about on the land and didn't need to stay near to the water.

One of the most important advances made by the reptiles was in the eggs they laid. Amphibians had jelly-coated eggs – like frogs' spawn – which they had to lay in water. The eggs hatched into tadpoles, which had to live in water as well. (Today's amphibians do just the same.) The tadpoles had to grow up and change into adults before they could crawl onto dry land.

The reptiles evolved an egg with a tough, waterproof shell. It could be laid anywhere – even in a desert. The young reptile had its own 'private pond' of water inside the shell, and a good supply of food in the form of *yolk*. The young reptile hatched out as a miniature version of its parents. The shelled egg set the reptiles free to become full-time land animals.

We know that these changes happened and how important they were, but skins, eggs and tadpoles are not often fossilized. We cannot usually directly say whether a certain fossil was amphibian or reptile. Instead we have to rely on features in the skeleton to distinguish between them.

Creature-catcher
Sauroctonus *was a primitive reptile from 250 million years ago. It grew to 3 metres long and its teeth were big and sharp – a sure sign that it was a meat-eater.*

The Dawn of the Age of Reptiles

1 Araeoscelis *was a lizard-like reptile about 30 cms in length. It probably fed on insects.*

2 Captorhinus *(30 cms long) was an early reptile from 300 million years ago. It had a heavy, solid skull and a clumsy body design, similar to its amphibian ancestors.*

3 Pareiasaurus *was one of the first plant-eating reptiles.*

4 Edaphosaurus *(3 metres in length), like its cousin* Dimetrodon*, had a sail on its back. Its blunt teeth tell us it ate plants – or perhaps shellfish.*

5 Dimetrodon *was a fierce meat-eater. Its fossils are very common in rocks from about 260 million years ago, as you can read on page 44.*

Amphibian or reptile?

Many of the differences between amphibians and reptiles are shown in the soft parts of their bodies – which aren't usually preserved as fossils. However, there are also some differences in their bones, which *are* preserved. These differences give us the clues we need to work out how amphibians gradually gave way to reptiles during the Permian. For example, in a reptile's spine two bones are joined to the hip bone. But in an amphibian's spine, only one bone is joined to the hip bone. There is also a difference in the bones of the hands and feet, as you can see on the left.

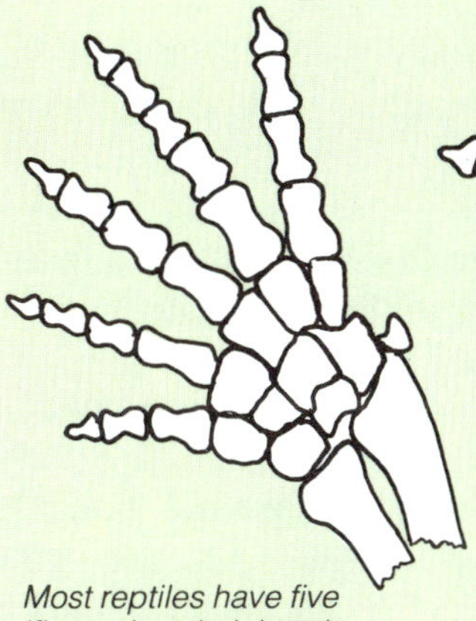

Most reptiles have five 'fingers' on their hands and feet. And some fingers are made up of five or even six bones.

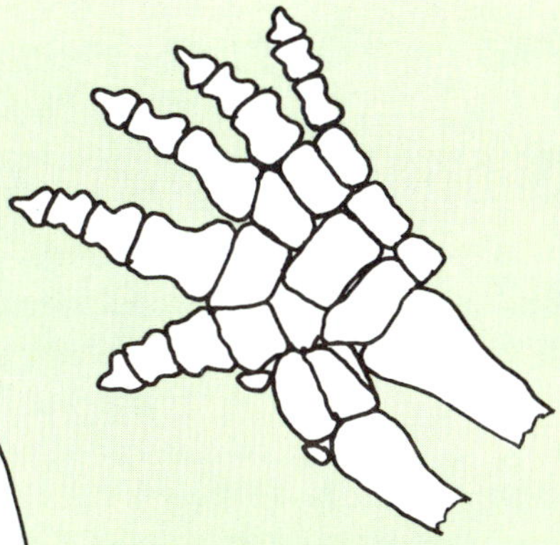

Many fossil amphibians, like their relatives today, have four 'fingers' or fewer on their hands and feet. Each finger is made up of only three or four bones.

Plant-crusher

Bradysaurus *was a slow-moving, plant-eating reptile of the middle Permian, that grew to 3 metres long. Its teeth were big and broad for crushing land vegetation.*

The first reptile?

One of the earliest reptiles yet discovered is *Hylonomus*, from over 300 million years ago. In 1852 many *Hylonomus* fossils were found in Nova Scotia in eastern Canada. The animals seem to have died curled up hidden in tree stumps, perhaps sheltering from a flood or other danger.

Many different types of reptiles appear in the fossil record soon after *Hylonomus*. It is unlikely that this creature was the ancestor of all of them. It was an early reptile – but probably not the first.

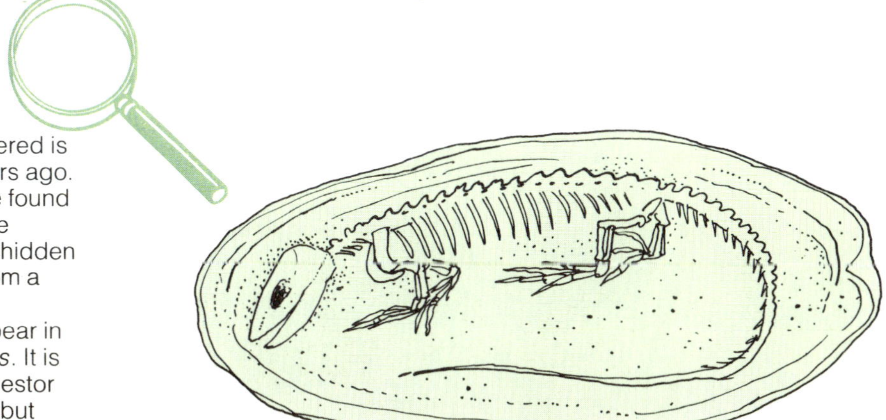

Sails in the sunrise

Some of the most interesting early reptiles belonged to a group called pelycosaurs. These can be thought of as very remote ancestors of humans, because they were on the side of the reptile 'family tree' that eventually led to the mammals (page 48).

The 'mammal-like' reptiles can be recognised by the single opening they have in the bones forming the side of the skull. Large numbers of fossilized pelycosaurs have been found in Texas, in rocks about 260 million years old. Some of these are very well preserved complete skeletons. Less complete remains are found in other parts of North America and Europe. The oldest pelycosaurs were mostly about a metre long, but they soon evolved to be 3 metres or more in length.

Some pelycosaurs were plant-eaters. They had flattened teeth, bulky bodies and small heads. *Cotylorhynchus* was one of the largest. The others were meat-eaters, and they had slim bodies, large heads and pointed teeth. *Dimetrodon* is one of the best known. It is the commonest fossil reptile found in the rocks from the early Permian period in Texas. Perhaps the most extraordinary thing about *Dimetrodon* was the enormous sail that ran down its back. This was made of skin supported by long spikes – each of which came from one bone in the spine. (The plant-eating pelycosaur *Edaphosaurus*, shown on page 41, had a similar sail.)

The most likely explanation for the sail is that it was an early attempt by reptiles to control their body temperature more effectively. A reptile's body works slowly and produces little heat. It depends on its surroundings for warmth, and in particular on heat from

All extras included!

Dimetrodon was one of the most advanced reptiles of its time, but it was not on the main line of reptile evolution. The dinosaurs and other great reptiles evolved from a separate group, the thecodonts (see page 49). *Dimetrodon* was able to warm up quickly in the morning with the help of its large, heat-absorbing sail. Other reptiles, still sluggish from the cold of the night, would be easy meat at this time of day.

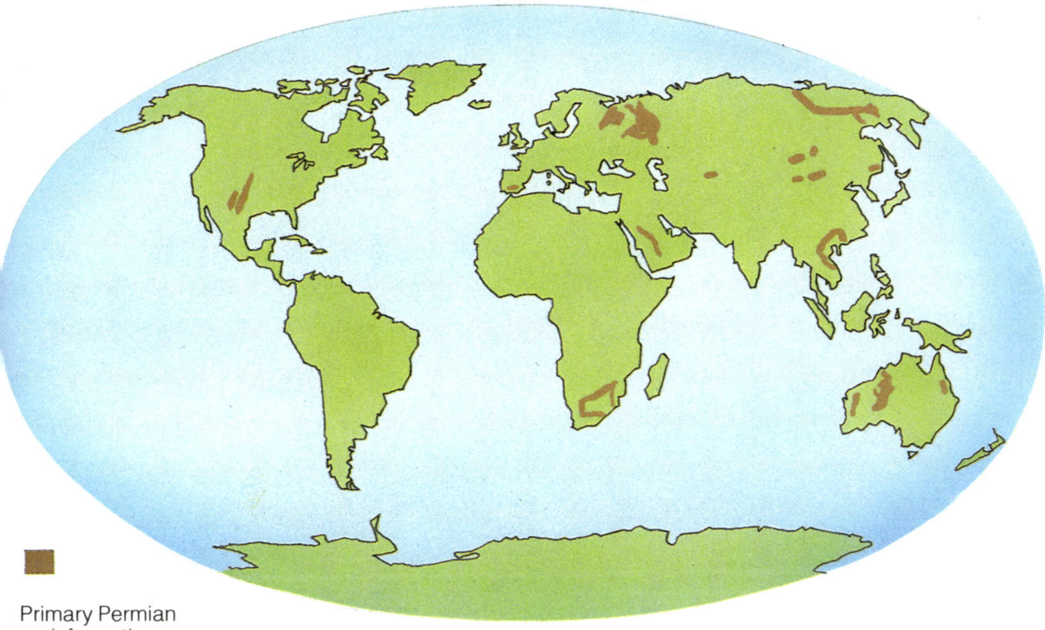

Primary Permian rock formations

From Perm to Texas
The Permian period was named in 1841 by the English geologist Roderick Murchison, after rocks found in the Perm region of the USSR. However much of today's knowledge about life during the Permian comes from the fossils such as Dimetrodon *which were found in the USA, mainly in Texas and other southern states.*

the Sun. Reptiles bask in the sun to get warmer and more active, or retreat into the shade if they are too hot.

A pelycosaur could sit sideways to the Sun in the early morning and soak up the warming rays, becoming active very quickly. In the heat of the day it could cool down by lying in the shade or sitting head-on to the Sun, so that only a little area of its body and sail was exposed. But by the middle of the Permian period the pelycosaurs themselves were disappearing, to be replaced by the therapsids (page 49).

No-frills pelycosaur
Varanosaurus *was a streamlined lizard-like pelycosaur about 1 metre long. Its fossils have been found in the Permian rocks of Texas.*

RADIATING REPTILES

In the relatively brief period called the Triassic, which lasted from 225 to 195 million years ago, there were rapid changes in reptile life. Many different types of reptile evolved or 'radiated' from the species previously alive in the Permian. Early in the Triassic the plant-eating dicynodonts flourished. Oddly, these reptiles were similar to the early mammals. They had two distinctive small tusks in the upper jaw, although many of them had no other teeth. Some were no bigger than a cat, while others were over 2 metres long. Their meat-eating cousins the cynognaths flourished early on but disappeared well before the end of the period.

The place of the cynognaths was taken by the first members of an up-and-coming group of reptiles known as archosaurs – the 'ruling reptiles'. The dinosaurs belonged to this group. However the first archosaurs were not dinosaurs, but reptiles called thecodonts.

Some thecodonts were shaped like clumsy crocodiles; others were slim, lightly-built and probably quite agile. Thecodonts such as *Euparkeria* could bring their legs under their bodies, instead of having legs sticking out at the side like the earlier reptiles. This seems to be the start of the successful body design found in their descendants, the dinosaurs.

By the end of the Triassic, the first true dinosaurs roamed the world. Soon they were evolving into every way of life imaginable. The dinosaur group of reptiles was about to dominate the land while other reptiles took to the sea and air.

Reptile evolution

This is an evolutionary tree showing the main groups of reptiles and their relatives. The first thing to notice is that not all the great reptiles were dinosaurs. The name dinosaur means 'terrible lizard' and was invented by Sir Richard Owen, the famous palaentologist, in 1841. But it is no longer an exact scientific term – it's now used more as a general name for any big, extinct land reptile.

The second thing to notice is that the reptiles' tree is not a neat one. It doesn't have all the extinct reptiles together in one group, leading to a single group of living reptiles. The living reptiles have evolved from different extinct reptiles. Two other very large groups – the mammals and the birds – are descended from separate lines of reptiles.

Thirdly, you can see that in the early stages of reptile evolution we aren't quite sure who is related to who. The thecodonts gave rise to many groups of reptiles, and also the birds, but exactly how this happened is not known. For the time being, until more fossils are discovered and the picture becomes clearer, scientists find it better to be fairly vague when they draw a tree like this – rather than try and be too accurate, and get it wrong!

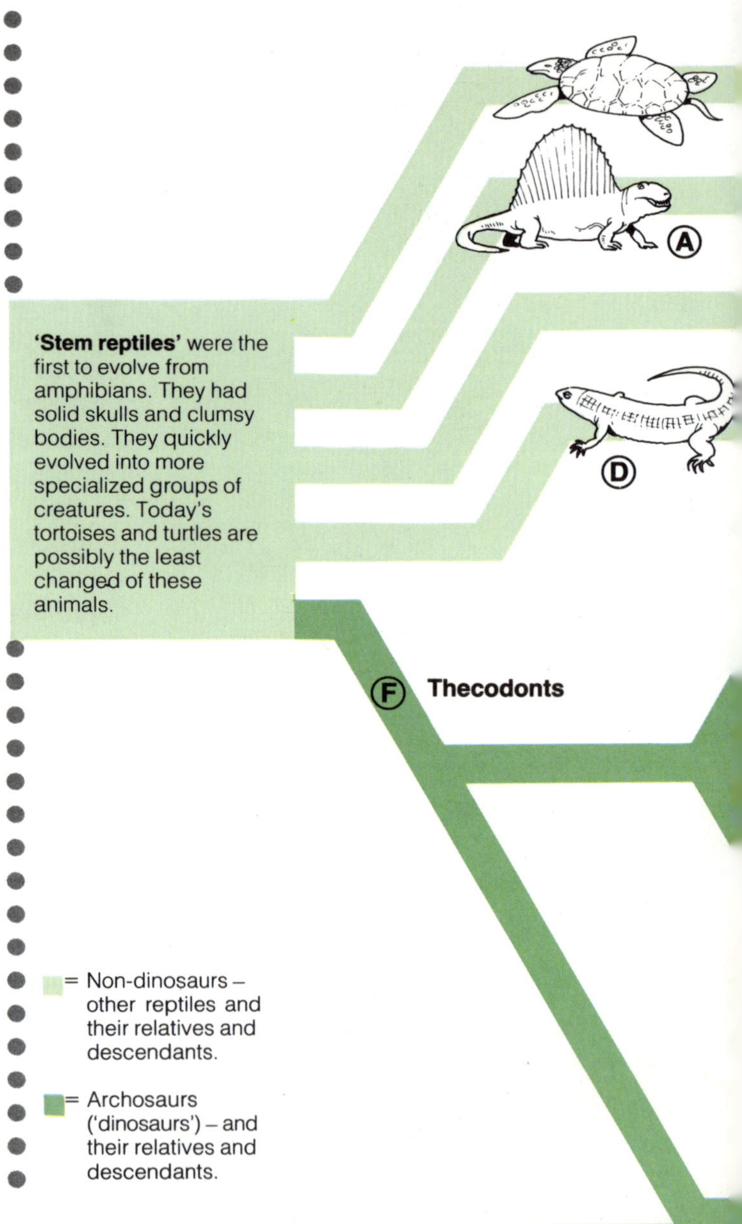

'Stem reptiles' were the first to evolve from amphibians. They had solid skulls and clumsy bodies. They quickly evolved into more specialized groups of creatures. Today's tortoises and turtles are possibly the least changed of these animals.

= Non-dinosaurs – other reptiles and their relatives and descendants.

= Archosaurs ('dinosaurs') – and their relatives and descendants.

Reptiles of the Triassic

1 Lystrosaurus *belonged to the reptile group known as dicynodonts. It was a tubby vegetarian and probably lived like the hippo does today, chomping water plants with its beak-like jaws.*

2 Euparkeria *was an agile reptile less than 1 metre long. It was a thecodont and could run well on all fours or on its back legs.*

3 Coelophysis *was one of the first dinosaurs. It may have used its long 'fingers' to grab its prey of small animals.*

4 Paradepedon *(2 metres in length), was a member of the herbivorous rhynchosaur group.*

5 Plateosaurus *was the first big dinosaur – growing to 8 metres long.*

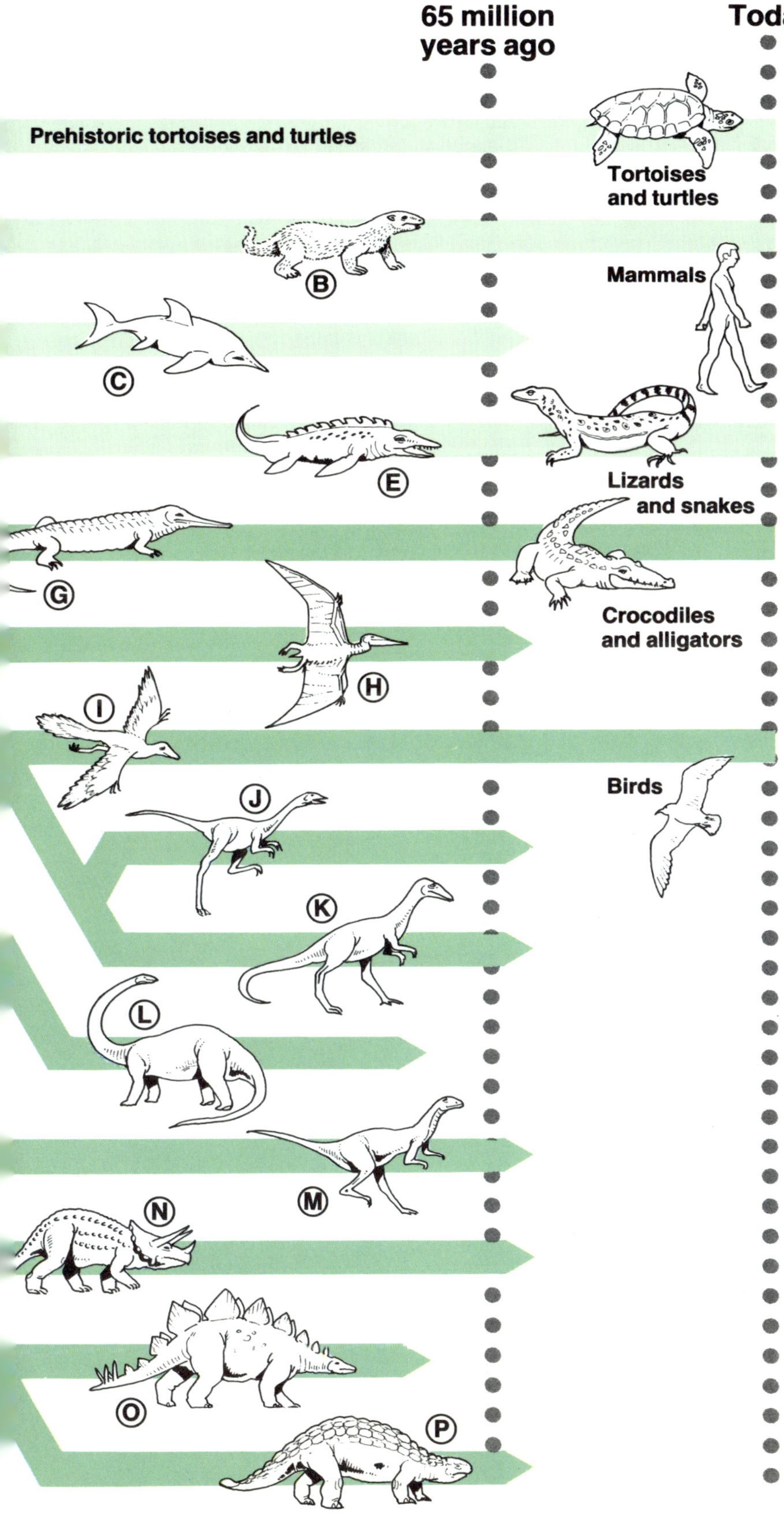

Ⓐ **Pelycosaurs** (mammal-like reptiles) were one of the first really successful reptile groups. Later they died out as the dinosaurs took over.

Ⓑ **Therapsids** were later mammal-like reptiles. When the dinosaurs disappeared the therapsids' mammalian descendants took over the world.

Ⓒ **Plesiosaurs and ichthyosaurs** were successful sea-going reptiles. Their line appeared about 200 million years ago, the placodonts being their early ancestors.

Ⓓ **Lepidosaurs** were prehistoric lizards, the distant ancestors of today's lizards and snakes. They evolved separately from the dinosaurs, about 250 million years ago. Lizards came first and snakes appeared about 100 million years ago.

Ⓔ **Mosasaurs** were large, fierce, sea-dwelling reptiles which had many similarities to lizards. Like other big reptiles they died out 65 million years ago.

Ⓕ **Thecodonts** were another group of 'stem reptiles'. In the beginning many were crocodile-like, but others soon evolved who were small and agile.

Ⓖ **Prehistoric crocodiles** first appeared about 200 million years ago. Some lived in the sea, others in fresh water. Crocodiles have remained much the same since.

Ⓗ **Pterosaurs** were flying reptiles that evolved some 200 million years ago. They developed long wings and a light body so that they resembled birds, but were in a separate group.

Ⓘ **Archaeopteryx** is the earliest bird yet discovered, from 147 million years ago. Birds probably evolved from the small meat-eating dinosaurs.

Ⓙ **'Ostrich dinosaurs'** were an offshoot of the meat-eating dinosaurs. They had toothless, beak-like jaws and the general shape of an ostrich with a long tail.

Ⓚ **Theropods** (meat-eating dinosaurs) stood on two legs, not four. They lived right through the Age of Dinosaurs and were very varied and successful.

Ⓛ **Sauropods** were the real giants – large, four-footed, plant-eating dinosaurs. The shape of their hips shows that they were probably related to meat-eating dinosaurs.

Ⓜ **Ornithopods** were two-legged herbivores. Some grew to a large size, others were small and fleet-footed. The 'duck-billed' dinosaurs were in this group.

Ⓝ **Ceratopsians** were horned dinosaurs with parrot-like beaks. They were successful towards the end of the Age of the Dinosaurs. Many were four-footed.

Ⓞ **Stegosaurs** were mostly large and four-footed. They appeared about 150 million years ago but became less common towards the end of the Age of Dinosaurs.

Ⓟ **Ankylosaurs** were medium-sized, four-footed dinosaurs with rather short legs. Their armour consisted of large bony plates in the skin.

How to say...

Lystrosaurus
Liss-trow-sore-us

Euparkeria
Ewe-parker-ear

Coelophysis
See-loff-izz-iss

Paradepedon
Para-dep-ee-don

Diplodocus
Dip-plod-owe-cuss

From field to laboratory

Fossils are found in all sorts of places, from seashores to high up in the mountains and from busy quarries to uninhabited deserts. The fossil expert has several tasks to carry out, once a fossil has been found. It must be carefully dug out of the rock, taken to the laboratory, cleaned up, repaired, and then studied. Some fossils are then exhibited to the public in museums.

Sometimes a mineralized fossil is harder than the surrounding rock. The fossil is left sticking out of its rock and it may sometimes be possible to pick up a whole fossil bone which is just lying on the ground.

Usually fossils are firmly embedded in the rock and have to be dug out. An embedded fossil is chipped free of as much rock as possible where it lies, so that it is easier to carry away. However, many fossils are too weak and fragile to dig out completely where they are found. In this case, a strengthening 'carrying case' is made around the fossils by coating them with plaster of Paris or a special hard-setting plastic foam before they are cut out.

In the laboratory the fossil is cut out of its man-made jacket, and then the rest of the rock is removed. In the old days a scientist had to chip away at the rock for hours on end with a hammer and chisel. This method is still used on tough specimens but there are now other ways of cleaning, as you can see on the right. The next thing to do is repair the fossil. A fossil bone may be in several pieces which need to be carefully glued together. Fossil skeletons often have parts of bones missing, but a skilled palaeontologist can reconstruct them.

Recovering fossils

Picking and drilling
Some fossil specimens are worked on with small high-powered drills, sanders and picks – rather similar to the tools used by dentists! The operator often watches his work through a magnifying lens or microscope.

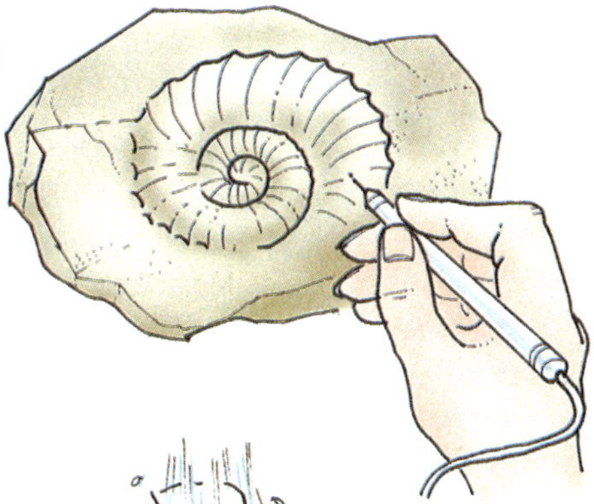

Sandblasting
If a small fossil is harder than the rock, it may be suitable for sandblasting. It is put in a small chamber and then grit or powder is blown at it under high pressure, which wears away the rock and leaves the fossil exposed.

Washing down
This method works on small fossils embedded in a rock – like chalk – that dissolves easily in water. The rock is put on the top of a tower of sieves, with the finest-mesh sieve at the base and the biggest-mesh one at the top. Water is then washed over the rock, which dissolves, and small fossils drop through the sieves.

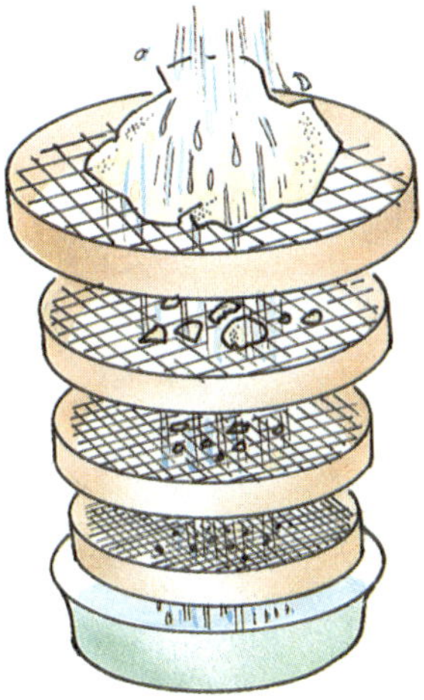

Acid bathing
This is only used on fossils embedded in some types of limestone, which can be dissolved away by acid much more quickly than the fossil. The specimen is given repeated dips in baths of different acids. In between dips, the acid is washed off and exposed parts of the fossil are painted with an acid resistant coating to protect them.

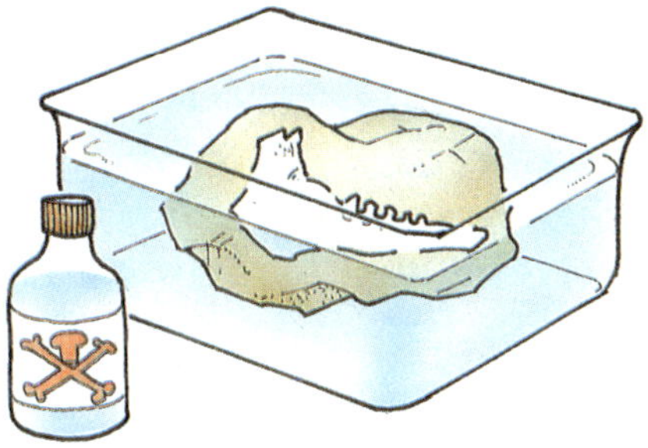

Discovery to display
1. *Palaeontologists discover and start to dig out fossil bones.*
2. *The fossils are set in plaster to protect them when they are carried.*
3. *One part of the find – a skull – is prepared for display in a laboratory.*
4. *The reconstruction is complete, and the whole fossil skeleton is displayed in a museum.*

THE DINOSAURS ARRIVE

By the Jurassic period, from 195 to 136 million years ago, the dinosaurs had truly arrived. Species of all shapes and sizes dominated the land.

One of the smallest dinosaurs, *Compsognathus*, lived in the Jurassic. It was a swift hunter the size of a chicken. The biggest dinosaurs, the giant sauropods, also lived in this period. They walked on all fours and had long necks and small heads. The giant among these giants was *Brachiosaurus*, which grew up to 12 metres tall and weighed 75 tonnes – far bigger than any land animal before or since. It would have been about the height of seven tall men standing on each other's shoulders!

As well as the big sauropods there were many other plant-eaters, often heavily armoured with rows of plates or spines down their backs. In addition there were huge meat-eaters – taller than a house – which could tackle their big prey.

There were no dinosaurs in the water but plenty of other reptiles lived there. Ichthyosaurs and plesiosaurs (page 61) chased their prey through the seas, while prehistoric crocodiles snapped up fish in rivers and lakes.

There are plenty of sea fossils from the first part of the Jurassic, but few fossils of land-dwelling creatures exist. However, the land animals of the later Jurassic are well known from fossils found in America and East Africa. Their remains give us a good idea of what the world was like during the Age of Dinosaurs.

How to say...

Compsognathus
Comp-sog-nay-thuss

Apatosaurus
Ap-at-owe-sore-us

Camptosaurus
Camp-tow-sore-us

Archaeopteryx
Ark-ee-op-ter-icks

Stenosaurus
Sten-owe-sore-us

The plant eaters

Dinosaurs found fossilized with their food inside them are very rare indeed. So the lifestyles of these animals and what they ate have to be deduced from tell-tale clues, such as the size and shape of their teeth, jaws, heads and bodies.

Most plant food is not very nourishing, and many plants are rather tough. This means plant-eaters (called *herbivores)* must eat large quantities in order to get enough nourishment. They also need large stomachs and intestines to help mash and digest the food. It's useful to have teeth and jaws that can cut or grind the plant food into small pieces, too. There is generally no need for a plant-eater to be very speedy, since plants don't run away! However it might be useful for a small plant-eater to be able to outrun a predator.

Working from these clues, we might expect a plant-eating dinosaur to be large-bodied, not particularly quick, and with a head and jaws adapted to gathering and eating plants.

The biggest of all dinosaur bodies belonged to the sauropods like *Diplodocus* and *Brachiosaurus*. These massive bodies could obviously hold plenty of food. But what about the 'gathering end'? Most sauropods had small heads compared to their body size. Their jaws were not very powerful either and their

Long body
Diplodocus, a sauropod, had a tiny head but a huge body. It must have spent nearly all its time eating. One skeleton measures nearly 27 metres long – the longest dinosaur yet discovered.

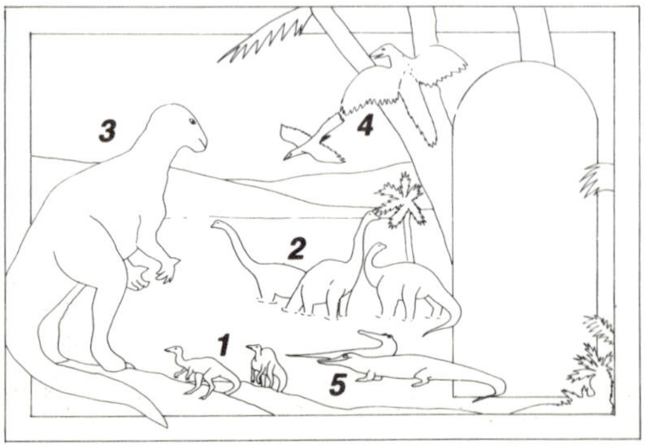

Dawn at a riverbank during the Jurassic

1 Compsognathus *lived about 140 million years ago. It snatched at its prey of small animals with its hands.*

2 Apatosaurus, *otherwise known as* Brontosaurus, *had a giraffe-like neck which suggests that it browsed on leaves high in trees.*

3 Camptosaurus *(4 metres long) was a 'hoofed dinosaur' and so probably walked on all fours.*

4 Archaeopteryx *(40 cms long) is a famous fossil. Often called the first bird, some scientists nowadays call it a 'feathered dinosaur'.*

5 Stenosaurus, *6 metres in length, lived in rivers and seas along with other giant crocodiles.*

Armoured plant-eaters
Triceratops *(left)* had *huge rows of teeth. This dinosaur may have chopped up palm fronds with its jaws to feed on the sap.*
Stegosaurus *(right) had jaws shaped like a beak and small leaf-like teeth to shred juicy plants. It probably fed on fairly soft, low-growing vegetation.*

teeth were rather feeble little pegs. Obviously these dinosaurs could not chew up tough plant food, so how could they deal with it?

The answer to this seems to be that some sauropods had gizzards, as birds do. The gizzard is like a 'pre-stomach'. It's a muscular bag into which swallowed food passes. It squeezes and squashes the food against hard things like pebbles or pieces of grit that the sauropod has also swallowed. Sauropod skeletons have been found with polished pebbles inside or close by. These pebbles may well have been swallowed by the dinosaur, to be churned around with the plant food. So from this we can guess that sauropods did indeed have gizzards, because the pebbles would have become polished as they ground up the food.

All those teeth!

Hadrosaurs like *Anatosaurus* lived towards the end of the Age of Dinosaurs, when many of the world's plants were similar to those of today. *Anatosaurus* seems to have fed on some of the toughest kinds of woody plant food. We know this because the *mummified* (dried-out) remains of one of these dinosaurs has been found with twigs, seeds and conifer needles in its stomach.

To cope with this diet the hadrosaur had amazing rows of teeth along the sides of its mouth. These teeth never stopped growing and being replaced (like those of most reptiles). *Anatosaurus* could have had 2,000 teeth in its mouth at the same time!

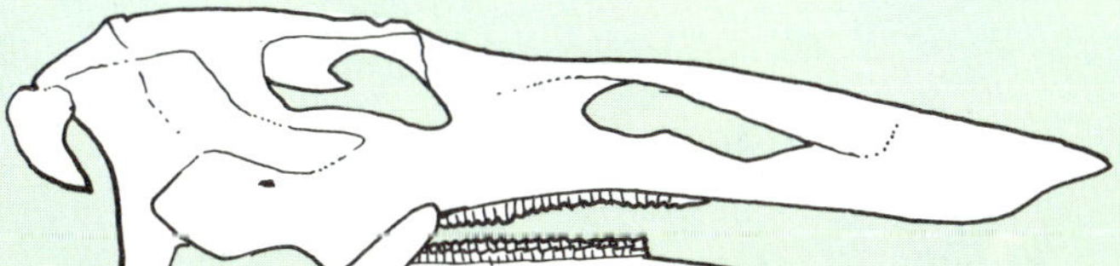

Anatosaurus skull

Dinosaur for dinner

Meat is a concentrated, nutritious food. Meat-eaters (called *carnivores*) generally don't need to consume huge quantities, and if they do have a large meal it may be some time before they need to eat again. So the body and intestines of a carnivore don't have to be especially big.

What a meat-eater does need, however, is the equipment to catch and cut up its prey. Many meat-eaters have good eyesight or a sensitive nose to help them find and track their meal. Their brains may well be quite large since they need flexible or 'intelligent' behaviour when hunting. Claws and teeth are usually big and sharp. Speed or agility may be necessary. The carnivorous dinosaurs showed many of these adaptations to the hunting way of life.

The 'tigers' of the dinosaur world were animals like *Allosaurus* – although at 12 metres long, this hunter was many times bigger than any tiger! Fossils show that its skull was light but large, 90 cms in length, and armed with ferocious, dagger-shaped teeth. These teeth had serrated edges, like saws. This creature's front and back feet had large, sharp claws. A predator like this would have been able to pounce and hold down its food with its claws, while at the same time slicing lumps of flesh with its teeth.

We do not know for certain what kind of prey *Allosaurus* took. It lived at the same time as huge sauropods such as *Diplodocus* and armoured dinosaurs

A fearsome foe
Allosaurus *lived about 150 million years ago. It used its long, heavy tail as a counterbalance as it strode along on two legs.*

A new meat eater!

This is the newly discovered dinosaur *Baryonyx walkeri*. This dinosaur's fossils were found in 1983, in a claypit in southern England. It was named *walkeri* after its discoverer, fossil collector William Walker. Its first name *Baryonyx* means 'heavy claw'. It had a huge claw – over a foot long – on each of its feet. It probably used the claw to spear its prey.

Baryonyx has been called the most important dinosaur discovery made in Europe this century, and differs from all other known dinosaurs. Experts at London's Natural History Museum spent three years working out what this creature – nicknamed 'Claws' – looked like. It would have grown up to 4½ metres tall and weighed around 2 tonnes.

Teeth and claws
Baryonyx had a long snout like an alligator's, with lots of small sharp teeth. Scientists could tell Baryonyx was a carnivore, and the snout is a clue that it ate fish. The experts think it speared the fish with its long sharp claws.

Bird-robber
Ornitholestes was a lightly-built carnivore about as tall as a human. Its name means 'bird robber'. Its fossil jaws are toothless which suggests that it probably had a horny beak like a bird, with which it snapped up insects and other small animals.

like *Stegosaurus*, so these may have been its prey. But like modern-day hunters it's likely that *Allosaurus* took whatever it could surprise.

The biggest carnivore of all time was *Tyrannosaurus*. It lived towards the end of the Age of Dinosaurs. This huge hunter was 12 metres long, 5 metres high and may have weighed around 7 tonnes. Its skull and jaws were very strongly built, possibly to cope with the struggles of its prey.

Tyrannosaurus used to be thought of as a slow-moving carrion feeder – meaning that it picked on dead and dying food. But its body shape and its skull and teeth tell us that it was an active animal. Fossils of its 'hands' have not been found, so these are usually reconstructed like its relation *Albertosaurus* which had two tiny fingers. What this huge, powerful dinosaur used its tiny arms for is still a puzzle. They were so short they couldn't even reach its mouth!

Discovering dinosaurs

People have been finding fossil dinosaur bones for many hundreds of years. But a long time ago no one knew what they were. Some people thought they were the bones of human giants. It was only about 160 years ago that people began to realise that these were the remains of giant, extinct reptiles.

In 1822 Gideon Mantell worked as a doctor in Sussex, in southern England. His hobby was geology (studying rocks). Apparently, one day his wife, while waiting for him to finish visiting a patient, discovered some large teeth in a heap of gravel at the roadside. Mantell traced the gravel to a certain quarry and there he found more fragments. But the teeth were unlike anything he had seen before. Even experts were no help. They assumed that the teeth belonged to a rhino or other large mammal.

At last Mantell met someone who had seen similar teeth, but much smaller, which belonged to the South American lizard *Iguana*. Mantell's idea that the fossil teeth were from a reptile seemed to be true. He invented the name *Iguanodon* ('iguana tooth') for their owner, who he thought was a giant lizard.

In 1824 another geologist, William Buckland, examined some fossil fragments including a jaw with teeth. He suspected they came from a huge meat-eating fossil reptile which he called *Megalosaurus*. Neither Buckland nor Mantell would have called these animals dinosaurs, as the word was not invented until 1841 (see page 48).

In 1858 dinosaur fossils were discovered in the United States. They were part of a *Hadrosaurus* skeleton.

Joseph Leidy made the first accurate reconstruction of a dinosaur. Soon after, people were able to make sense of the 'giant bird' tracks that had been found in Massachusetts as long ago as 1802. They were in fact dinosaur footprints.

A huge number of dinosaur discoveries were made in North America in the later part of the nineteenth century. This was partly due to the rivalry between two fossil collectors, Edward Cope and Charles Marsh. In 20 years from about 1870 to 1890 they found over 130 new kinds of dinosaur. Soon dinosaur fossils were found in other countries. *Brachiosaurus* was discovered in Tanzania, and dinosaur eggs were uncovered in Mongolia (page 66). Dinosaur fossils have now been found almost all over the world.

The best known dinosaur

Iguanodon, besides being one of the first dinosaurs ever discovered, is also very famous. In 1878 a huge collection of fossil *Iguanodon* skeletons was found in a mine in Belgium. The scene at the discovery must have looked like that shown in the old print on the left. Scientists spent years studying the bones – as did many other interested museum visitors (below, left). Now we know this ornithopod dinosaur better than almost any other. It lived about 115 million years ago and grew up to 9 metres long. *Iguanodon* (shown alive, below) probably ate plants, which it cut off with the hard, beak-like front of its mouth. It then crushed the food with the grinding teeth at the back of its mouth.

REPTILES OF THE SEAS

During the time that the dinosaurs ruled the land, other reptiles took over the seas. One group that flourished briefly in the Triassic period were the placodonts. They had flat teeth for crushing shellfish and some were armour-plated like turtles. Fossils of the first true turtles have been found dating from the Triassic. By the end of the Age of Dinosaurs, turtles were similar to today's – but much bigger, with some growing to be over 4 metres long.

Ichthyosaurs were common sea-dwelling reptiles in the Jurassic period. Their name means 'fish-lizards' and they had a fish-like fin in the middle of their backs and a large tail to thrust them through the water. Their limbs had evolved into steering paddles. Plesiosaurs were another group of marine reptiles that lived in the Jurassic seas. They had large paddle-shaped limbs which they used to row themselves through the water. *Mosasaurus* was yet another giant sea reptile, from the late Cretaceous. This was a huge relation of today's monitor lizard and had ferocious rows of sharp teeth.

Not all the creatures shown here lived at the same time. Nevertheless, during the Age of Reptiles few sea creatures were safe from these predatory marine reptiles. But it was all to no avail. When the end came for the land dinosaurs and their flying cousins, the sea reptiles went with them.

How to say...

Archelon
Ark-ay-lon

Placodus
Plack-owe-dus

Henodus
Hen-owe-dus

Ichthyosaurus
Ikth-ee-owe-sore-us

Cryptoclidus
Crip-tow-clide-us

Success or failure?

People often use the word dinosaur to mean something which is big, old and a failure! But were the dinosaurs really failures?

In the sense that they became extinct, while other creatures like the mammals survived, they did fail. However this may have been due to some very unusual changes in the world around them. If such drastic changes happened today, many mammals would die out.

It is impossible to say what might have happened had the dinosaurs lived on. We do know that, right up to the time of their extinction 65 million years ago, they still seemed to be successful. They dominated the land and were still evolving into new and improved forms, right to their sudden end.

Dinosaurs have sometimes been called stupid or slow-witted. Some perhaps were. *Stegosaurus*, for example, had an amazingly small brain for its size. Its brain was only 3 cms long while the body was 6 metres long! But many of the other dinosaurs, as far as fossils tell us, did not have especially small brains. In fact some of the small meat-eaters like *Stenonychosaurus* had large brains and may have been quite intelligent.

There is much argument about whether dinosaurs were cold-blooded, like today's reptiles, or warm-blooded, that is able to keep their bodies at a constant temperature, like birds and mammals. The inside of some fossil dinosaur bones looks like the inside of mammal bones, which some scientists

Brains, not brawn
Stenonychosaurus *lived about 80 million years ago. Its large head contained a big brain in proportion to its body, which was only 1½ metres long. It may well have been a fairly clever hunter, tricking or trapping its prey.*

Mammal ancestor
Megazostrodon *fossils have been found in southern Africa. This early mammal lived at a time when the dinosaurs were only just beginning their reign.*

Ocean dwellers of the Age of Reptiles

1 Archelon *was up to 4 metres long and weighed 3 tonnes, making it the largest turtle known.*

2 Placodus *lived in shallow seas. and on the shores. It grew to over 2 metres long and fed on shellfish.*

3 Henodus *(1 metre long), a placodont, is from Triassic seas. It resembled a turtle but it was not a close relative.*

4 Ichthyosaurus *was one of the best-known 'fish-lizards' and was about 3 metres long. It hunted in groups, preying mainly on belemnites whose shells are preserved inside some fossil ichthyosaurs.*

5 Cryptoclidus *3 metres long, was a plesiosaur. Some people who believe in the 'Loch Ness Monster' think it may be a plesiosaur just like this one!*

say is evidence for their warm-bloodedness. Other scientists say that a large dinosaur in what we think was a warm climate would be warm most of the time anyway. For the time being the arguments go on and no one can say for sure.

But in one respect, as far as we know, all dinosaurs were 'primitive'. They laid eggs. They did not give birth to live young, like most mammals. Neither did they have certain physical and behavioural 'improvements' that went with giving birth. In this respect the dinosaurs fell behind the reptiles' other evolutionary line, the therapsids (page 49).

Dinosaur look-alikes

Some dinosaurs were very similar in body size and shape to animals in the world today. For example in general build *Hypsilophodon* had similarities with an antelope, while *Palaeoscinus* resembled an armadillo. These resemblances were due to them evolving in similar surroundings and leading similar ways of life to their look-alikes today. Similarities like this are called *evolutionary convergence*.

Hypsilophodon

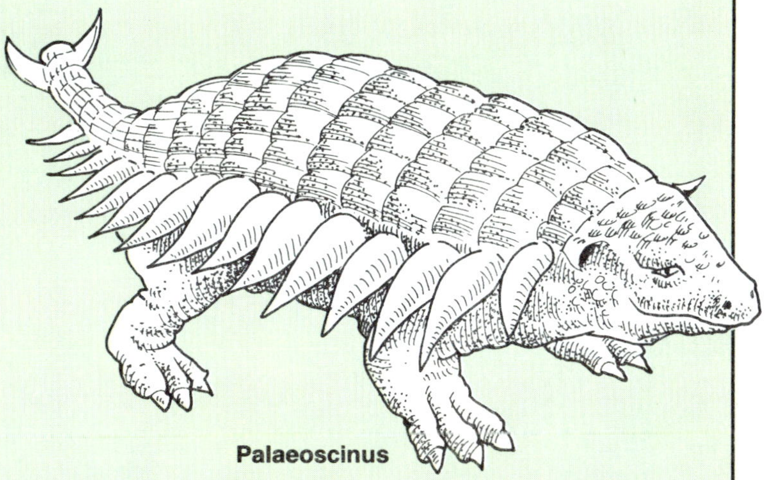

Palaeoscinus

DINOSAUR HEYDAY

The heyday of the dinosaurs was during the Cretaceous period, from 136 to 65 million years ago. Dinosaurs covered the land in greater variety and with more advanced designs than ever before. The big four-footed sauropods still walked the Earth, but as time went by they began to die out and new types of plant-eaters took their place. *Iguanodon* was one of these.

At the beginning of the Cretaceous the warm, wet landscape was very different to the one we know today. Large plants such as seed-ferns and cycads had been around for a long time, but new types of plant were slowly taking over. These were flowers and trees – familiar to us today. Grasses, however, had not yet evolved and so there were no wide, open, grassy plains.

By the end of the Cretaceous many recognisable plants and animals were living on the Earth. Oak and magnolia trees were common, ducks and herons lived on the lakes and rivers. The dinosaurs were adapting well, and near the end of the Cretaceous there was a huge array of species. Plant-eaters included the duck-bills, four-legged armoured dinosaurs and horned dinosaurs. These herbivores provided food for many meat-eaters such as the largest carnivore ever to walk the land – the Cretaceous dinosaur *Tyrannosaurus*. Who would have guessed that within a few million years every single dinosaur, and most other large reptiles, would have gone forever?

How to say...

Corythosaurus
Corry-thow-sore-us

Tyrannosaurus
Ty-ran-owe-sore-us

Styracosaurus
Sty-rack-owe-sore-us

Deinonychus
Day-non-ee-cus

Ornithomimus
Ore-nith-owe-mime-us

Triceratops
Try-cerra-tops

Family life

We can only guess the answers to many of the questions we have about how dinosaurs lived. Did they live in groups? Did they look after their young? Did males and females look different? How did they breed? We will probably never know the truth about most dinosaurs. Just occasionally, though, fossils give us a fascinating glimpse into the past and we can answer some of these questions for a particular kind of dinosaur.

Hollow nests

Fossil nests of the small dinosaur *Protoceratops* have been found in Mongolia. These nests were hollows that the dinosaur dug in the sand. Inside the nests were about 12 eggs, which were arranged in a kind of spiral, as they were laid. Fossils of this dinosaur have been discovered in various stages of growth, from hatchling to adult. We now know how *Protoceratops* changed in size and shape as it grew.

An American/Asian scene during the Cretaceous

1 Corythosaurus, *which grew to 13 metres in length, was a 'duck-billed' dinosaur.*

2 Tyrannosaurus, *the largest meat-eater ever, had dagger-like teeth up to 15 cms long, with which it killed and slashed at its prey.*

3 Styracosaurus *(5 metres long) had an impenetrable array of horns on its armour-plated head. It ate plants.*

4 Deinonychus *stood just taller than a human. It probably used the ferocious claws on its second toes to slash at its prey.*

5 Ornithomimus *was one of the 'ostrich dinosaurs'.*

6 Triceratops *was one of the last dinosaurs. They were alive up to the point of the great extinction, 65 million years ago.*

Herds and tracks

Sometimes many dinosaurs of one type are found together. This can lead scientists to deduce that they were a herd struck down by tragedy. On the other hand such 'herds' may be bones that collected over a period of time, perhaps washed together each year by a flood.

Tracks showing 20 or more dinosaurs all moving through the same area, in the same direction, are good evidence of herds. *Iguanodon* tracks, shown here, often show several animals apparently moving together. From what we know of large plant-eating animals today, like zebras or antelopes, it would seem very likely that some herbivorous dinosaurs did live in groups. This would give them some protection from large meat-eaters.

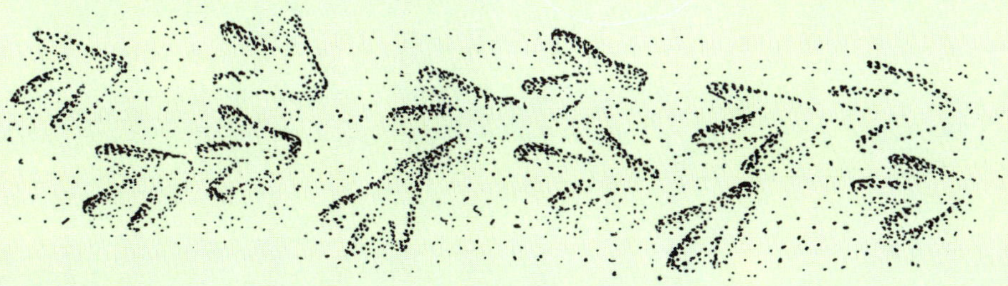

Mums and dads

Did male and female dinosaurs look different? From what we know of present-day reptiles, the answer is probably yes. It is difficult to spot the difference in fossils, but it is sometimes possible. Two types of Iguanodon *have been found in Europe. One was larger and more heavily built than the other. They could be different species, but some scientists think that they were males and females of the same species.*

Nesting like birds?

Perhaps the most interesting fossil nest found belongs to the hadrosaur *Maiasaurus*. These dinosaurs made nests with a mud rim and, after hatching, the young seem to have stayed in the nest for a while. We know this because in addition to hatchling-sized young, remains of other, larger youngsters have been found in fossil nests. These had worn teeth, which would seem to show that the young were fed in the nest by their parents, as birds do today.

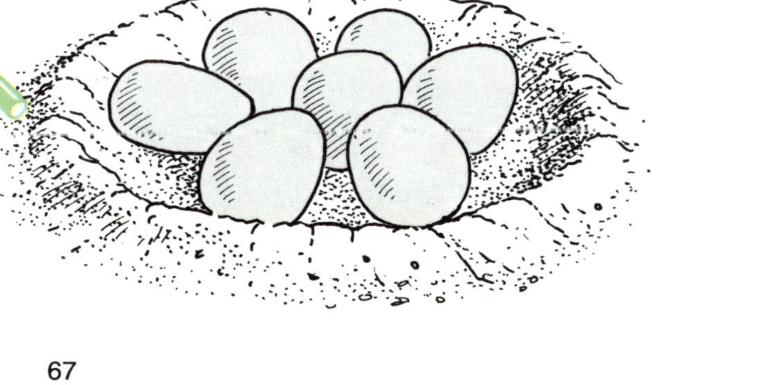

The reptiles take off

Several different kinds of reptile have taken to the air. The modern 'flying dragon' lizard glides from tree to tree on 'wings' of stretched skin. Over 200 million years ago *Kuhneosaurus* was gliding and it had better wings than its modern relation. But gliding like this is not true flying, it's only an addition to a mainly earthbound life. The reptiles which really mastered the air – other than those that evolved into birds – were the pterosaurs.

Pterosaurs, like dinosaurs, evolved from a group of lightly-built archosaurs (page 47). In some ways their bodies became very similar to those of birds, but pterosaurs had developed quite separately.

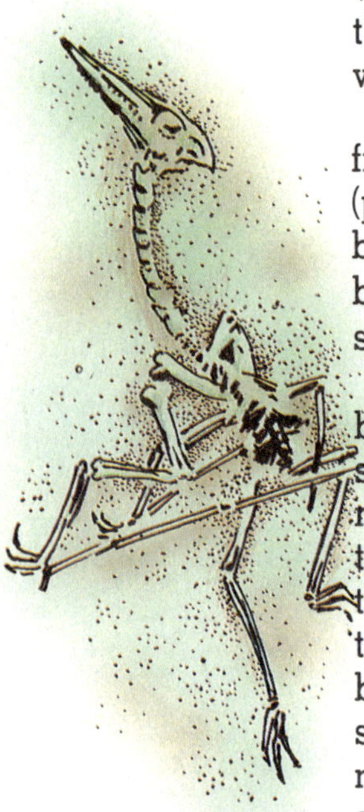

Giant scavenger?
In 1972 the remains of huge Quetzalcoatlus, *were discovered. They are not complete, but they indicate a creature like* Pteranodon *– yet much larger, with a wingspan of 15 metres! This monster seems to have lived over land, not sea, and may have scavenged like a modern vulture.*

In pterosaurs, the front limbs became wings. The arm and hand stayed much the same as in other reptiles, but the main difference was in the fingers. Three of these stuck out at the front, while the fourth finger was the extraordinary one. Each of its bones became enormously long, to support the wing itself. The wing was made of leathery skin, not feathers, and its outline can be seen clearly in some fossils.

Many old pictures of what scientists thought pterosaurs looked like, show the wing attached to the hind limb. However this is no longer certain. Also, pterosaurs used to be thought of only as gliders, swooping above the sea in which they fished, then returning to cliffs or islands to roost. Scientists used to think that a pterosaur's muscles were not strong enough for flapping, that the creature was too clumsy to move on land, and that it could only take off by jumping from a tree or cliff.

But as pterosaurs are studied more closely and more fossil discoveries are made, it now seems quite likely that none of these things are true. Pterosaurs may have been just as good at flying as birds. Being active, flying creatures they might even have been warm-blooded. Several scientists suggested that pterosaurs may have had fur, to keep themselves warm, and some experts thought they could see traces of hair on fossils. In 1970 a Russian scientist discovered remains of the pterosaur *Sordes* with what looked very much like a furry covering.

All sizes of pterosaur

Some pterosaurs were very small. Pterodactylus *of 150 million years ago was only the size of a starling. It may have caught insects with its small teeth while flying.*

Others were bigger. Rhamphorhynchus *from 140 million years ago had a wingspan of 1½ metres. Its long tail probably helped to balance it and acted as a rudder as it changed direction in mid-air. It had pointed teeth and may have been a fish-eater.*

Some pterosaurs, like the giant Pteranodon *that lived 80 million years ago, were toothless. It had a wingspan of over 7 metres and may well have been the pterosaur equivalent of the albatross, spending long periods gliding effortlessly over the ocean.*

Fitted out for flying

Many parts of a pterosaur's body were designed for flight, just like a bird of today. Can you see any other similarities between pterosaurs and birds?

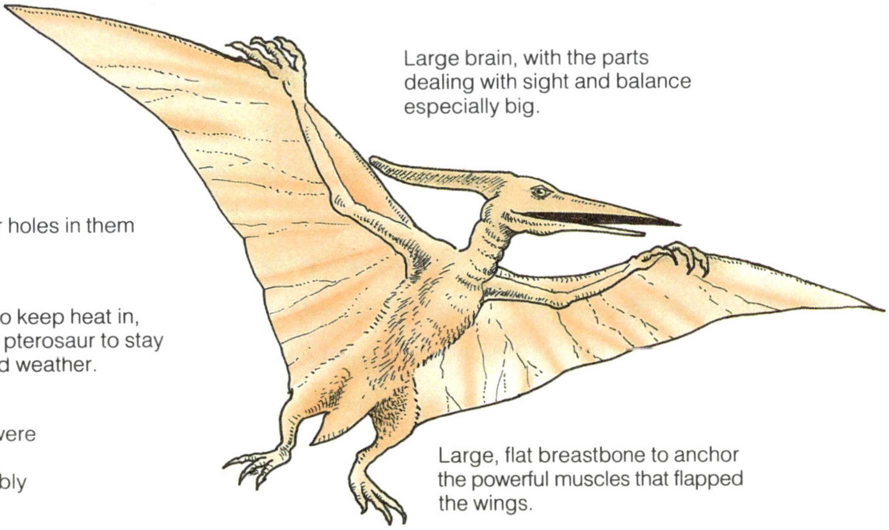

Helmets, spines & armour

Large slow-moving animals need protection against predators. For many dinosaurs this protection took the form of some sort of armour-plating. Fossilized dinosaur skin has been found with large, tough scales in it. The same type of tough skin with bony plates in it can be seen in the dinosaurs' present-day relatives, the crocodiles. But in some dinosaurs the protective armour was much more elaborate.

In the ankylosaur group of dinosaurs, like *Euoplocephalus*, the whole back was armoured with strong knobs of bone set into the skin. Strong bony plates covered the head and spines stuck out from the neck and shoulders. Smaller spines went down the back to the base of the tail. The tail itself had large, strong bones and on its end was a huge club made of plates of bone welded together in the skin. This dinosaur tail would have been a very powerful weapon when swung against any hungry meat-eaters.

The slow-moving *Stegosaurus* also had armour. This was made up of bony plates along its back. The plates were apparently arranged alternately, starting with small ones behind the head and increasing in size to the hip and base of the tail. The end of the tail had spines. A few scientists have suggested that these bony plates lay flat on the dinosaur's back, but most believe they were upright.

In the upright position the plates could have had another use besides protection. Skin-covered plates of this size and position could have helped to absorb heat when cold or lose it when hot (like the *Dimetrodon's* sail shown on page 41). The fossilized bony plates have many little grooves in them, which could have had small blood vessels running through them. This would increase the efficiency of the plates as coolers or warmers.

Plated for protection
The ankylosaur Euoplocephalus *was so well armoured that it even had hard, bony plates in its eyelids!*

The call of the wild

Some of the 'duck-billed' dinosaurs had crests on their heads. But fossils show that the crest was not solid bone. It was hollow, usually with air passages from the nostrils to the throat passing through it. Perhaps it was used as a vibrating or resonating chamber, to make the dinosaur's calls louder. Modern alligators make extremely loud booming calls at mating time. So prehistoric reptiles may well have done the same. A dinosaur like *Parasaurolophus* which was 10 metres long, had a crest 1 metre long. If this resonated when the dinosaur made its call, the sound could have been heard miles away!

Head-banging
The male Stegoceras *may have used its thick, strong head to butt rival males at breeding time, as in the picture below. The winner of the competition would get to mate with the females. This dinosaur belonged to a group called the 'dome-heads'.*

Keeping it cool
The plates along the back of Stegosaurus *could have helped control body temperature as well as acting as protection.*

Alfred Wegener
German explorer and geology theorist, Wegener first put forward the idea of 'continental drift' in 1915.

The changing world of the dinosaur

Animals and plants were not the only things to evolve and change during the Age of the Dinosaurs. The land under the dinosaurs' feet was itself changing and moving.

We tend to think of the Earth and its continents as being fixed. In fact the continents are gradually creeping across the Earth's surface, to take up new positions.

They have been on the move since well before the time of the dinosaurs. When dinosaurs first appeared the landmasses of the Earth had all come together in a 'supercontinent' that scientists have called Pangaea. Over millions of years this split up and the pieces moved into the positions familiar to us from maps and photographs today.

The idea of 'continental drift' was first suggested in 1915 by Alfred Wegener, who noticed the jigsaw fit between the continents in their outlines and rock formations. At this time his ideas were rejected but today they are assumed to be true. Scientists have only recently been able to carry out research and make measurements to explain how the continents move.

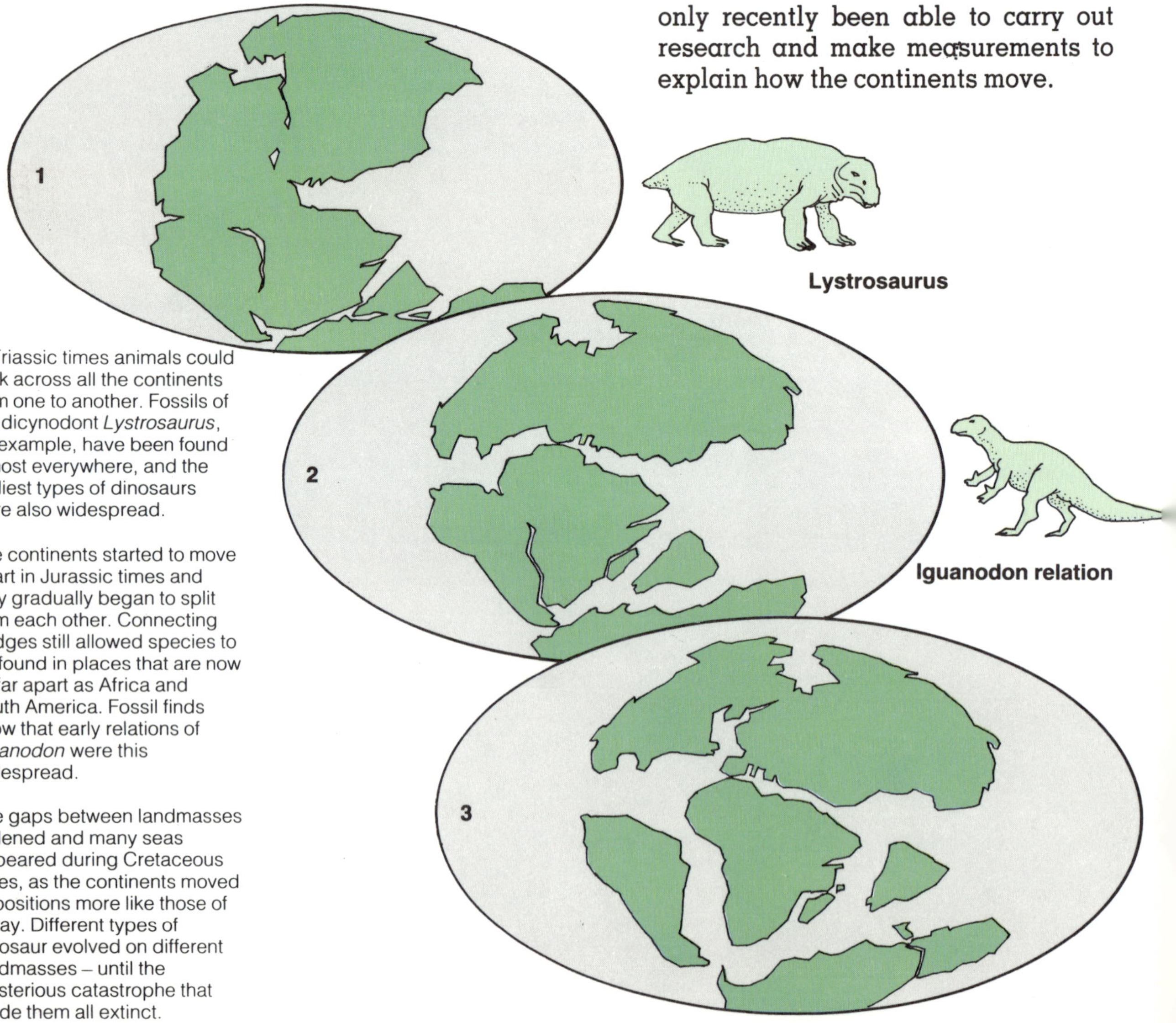

Lystrosaurus

Iguanodon relation

1 In Triassic times animals could walk across all the continents from one to another. Fossils of the dicynodont *Lystrosaurus*, for example, have been found almost everywhere, and the earliest types of dinosaurs were also widespread.

2 The continents started to move apart in Jurassic times and they gradually began to split from each other. Connecting bridges still allowed species to be found in places that are now as far apart as Africa and South America. Fossil finds show that early relations of *Iguanodon* were this widespread.

3 The gaps between landmasses widened and many seas appeared during Cretaceous times, as the continents moved to positions more like those of today. Different types of dinosaur evolved on different landmasses – until the mysterious catastrophe that made them all extinct.

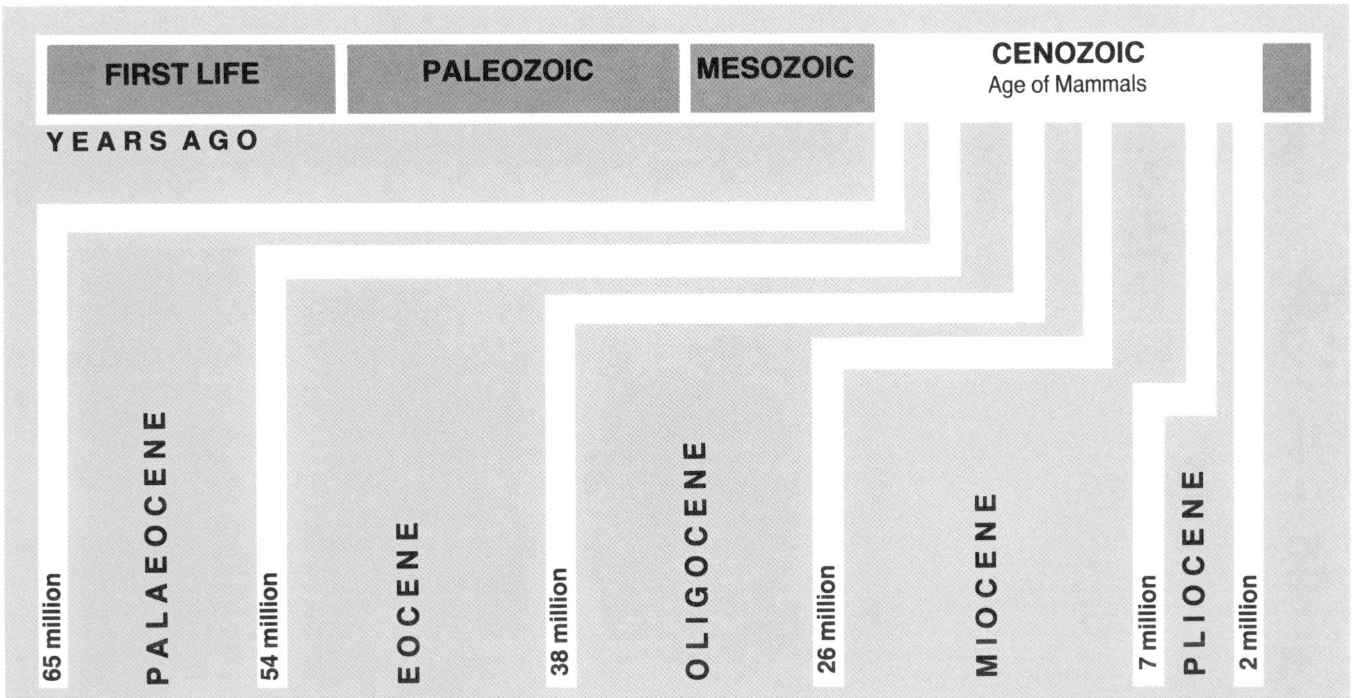

PART THREE

MIGHTY MAMMALS OF THE PAST

The death of the dinosaurs made way for a whole new group of creatures – a group that was to step forward from the sidelines to take a central place in the history of the Earth and its inhabitants. That group was the mammals, the first creatures to give birth to live young. From tiny mice to gigantic mammoths, they succeeded the dinosaurs to begin a new age in the development of our planet.

THE FIRST MAMMALS

Sixty-five million years ago, dinosaurs suddenly became extinct. How suddenly we may never know. It was quick in terms of the fossil record in the rocks, but it happened so long ago that it's almost impossible for us to tell if they died out over a few months or thousands of years.

What is certain is that the dinosaurs, which had been the biggest, most successful and probably the brainiest animals to live on this planet for more than 100 million years, were completely wiped out. Many other living things also died, including over half the plants and lots of the surface-dwelling sea creatures. But some things managed to survive, and the disappearance of the dinosaurs provided them with a great opportunity to take over the Earth. The creatures that took this opportunity were the mammals.

Mammals were already around during and even before the Age of Dinosaurs. But they were mostly small, nocturnal animals that spent their time scampering through the undergrowth or climbing trees in order to hide from the hunting dinosaurs. Mammals seemed to have no way of challenging the dinosaurs for supremacy. But once the dinosaurs disappeared, they got their chance. Mammals quickly took over the land and became the dominant animals. The last 65 million years – and perhaps the next few million – are all part of the Age of Mammals.

Iridium in clay
In the photo above you can see the clay layer containing iridium (marked by a coin) that was formed during the Cretaceous period and discovered by scientists just a few years ago.

Death by meteorite

A layer of clay, containing a lot of the rare metal iridium, has been discovered in various parts of the Earth's crust. This has led scientists to believe that a huge meteorite – estimated to be 10 kms across – may once have crashed into our planet, as iridium is rare on Earth but common in meteorites. The dust and rocks thrown into the air when it crashed, would have stopped heat and light from the Sun reaching the Earth, and may have led to the death of the dinosaurs.

Why did the dinosaurs disappear?

What could have happened 65 million years ago to kill the dinosaurs? There are many suggestions, but some of them are difficult to believe. One theory says the dinosaurs were too stupid to survive, but modern evidence shows they were the most advanced creatures of their time. Some had large brains and were probably quite clever. Another explanation is that disease wiped them out – but it's hard to imagine a disease which could affect so many different kinds of animal all at once.

One big problem is that the theory must explain not just the death of the dinosaurs, but the disappearance of many other kinds of animals and plants too. At the same time as the dinosaurs were dying, so were most of the large non-dinosaur reptiles that lived on the land. Pterodactyls, some kinds of plants and sea creatures also vanished.

The most likely explanation for all this death and destruction is that there were great changes in climate. It is possible that a massive meteorite crashed into the Earth, throwing up huge clouds of dust that blotted out the Sun. Another theory is that the dinosaurs died out over a much longer period, as a result of normal changes to the climate and also

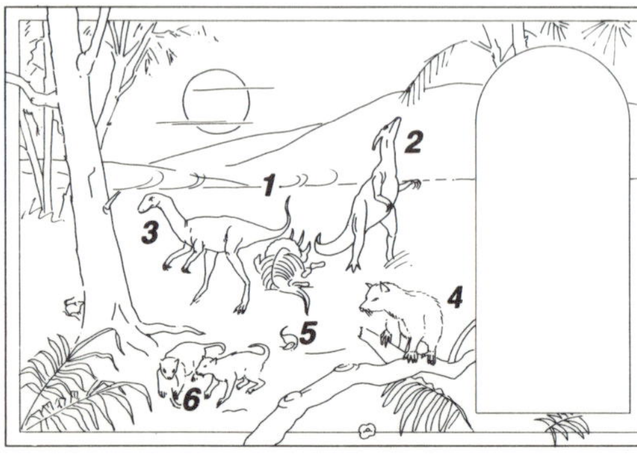

North America at the end of the Age of Dinosaurs

1 Triceratops *was a plant-eating dinosaur that grazed in herds.*

2 Thescelosaurus *was another plant-eating dinosaur – a new type that appeared near the end of the Age of Dinosaurs.*

3 Stenonychosaurus *was a meat-eating dinosaur about the size of a human being. It may have hunted small mammals at night.*

4 Didelphodon *was a marsupial similar to today's opossums.*

5 *Insect-eating mammals resembling today's shrews lived alongside the dinosaurs for millions of years.*

6 *Many small plant-eating mammals belonged to the group called multituberculates, but became extinct as more modern mammals appeared.*

changes in the sea level. Some scientists have looked for a connection with the amount of heat and light coming from the Sun which could have made the dinosaurs too cold or too hot. A few have suggested that our Sun has a twin, which usually remains hidden behind the normal Sun, but comes out every now and again to overheat the Earth.

You may have guessed by now that the real truth is that we do not know what caused the death of the dinosaurs and the other animals and plants! We may never find out for sure, but digging up clues and piecing together evidence is certainly exciting work.

A cooling climate

65 million-year old fossils found in Montana, USA, show the Earth's climate changed a lot over half a million years.

The fossils show us that warm sub-tropical forests, like the one below, which were home for lots of dinosaurs, became replaced with cool pine forests and a completely different mixture of animals. This may have happened due to changes in the climate caused by the continents drifting and altering sea levels.

How to say...

Triceratops
Try-serra-tops

Thescelosaurus
Thes-kell-oh-sore-us

Stenonychosaurus
Sten-on-iko-sore-us

Didelphodon
Die-dell-fow-don

Did they all die?

If cold killed the dinosaurs, perhaps a few survived where the climate stayed warm – in parts of tropical Africa, for example. Most scientists cannot believe that there are still a few dinosaurs alive on the Earth, but even today there are stories of unknown beasts living in remote swamps, and huge creatures hiding away in the depths of dark lagoons. Could it be that they are the last survivors of the Age of Dinosaurs?

Too hot for comfort

Some fossil dinosaur eggs from late in the Age of Dinosaurs have been found to have extremely thin shells.

Nowadays, birds lay thin-shelled eggs if they are diseased, poisoned or if the climate around them is too hot. Was this the case for the dinosaurs? Perhaps the Earth became very hot – due to the appearance of another Sun, or our Sun becoming very active.

If this happened, the increase in temperature would have killed the dinosaurs, since they were unable to cool themselves, and it would also have affected the sea-dwelling creatures.

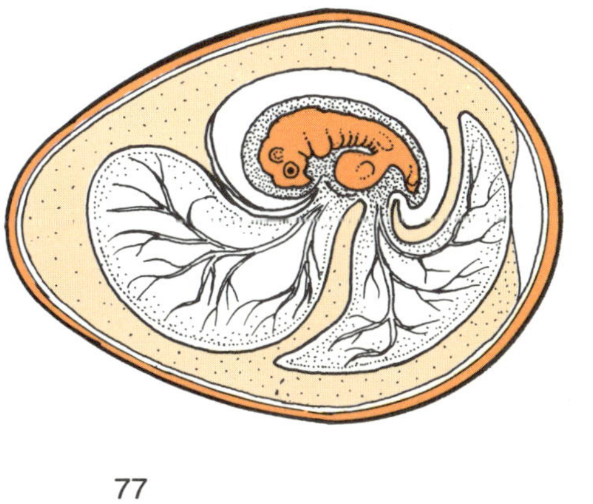

The first mammals

We may not know why the dinosaurs died out. But do we know why mammals took over? Before we can answer that question, we must decide what a mammal is. The main features to look out for are shown on the right. Most important is the fact that mammals are warm-blooded. They keep their bodies at a constant temperature, and are ready for action at all times, and in all weather. The reptiles (including the dinosaurs) were cold-blooded and needed to soak up heat energy from the sun before they could move about. Lots of them were very big so they absorbed heat slowly, but once they became warm they had no way of cooling themselves down if the climate became too hot. This could be why the mammals survived 65 million years ago while the dinosaurs perished through overheating or by being frozen to death.

Although fossils can't tell us if a prehistoric animal was warm-blooded, they do give us a few clues. By looking at an animal's bones – the main parts usually preserved as fossils – we can often work out whether or not it was a mammal.

You can see from the chart below that scientists have found a whole series of fossil animals which gradually change from reptiles to mammals. We must draw a line somewhere and say: "All animals with these features are mammals." Most fossil experts agree that if an animal is found to have a single bone for its lower jaw and three small bones in each ear, then we can call it a mammal.

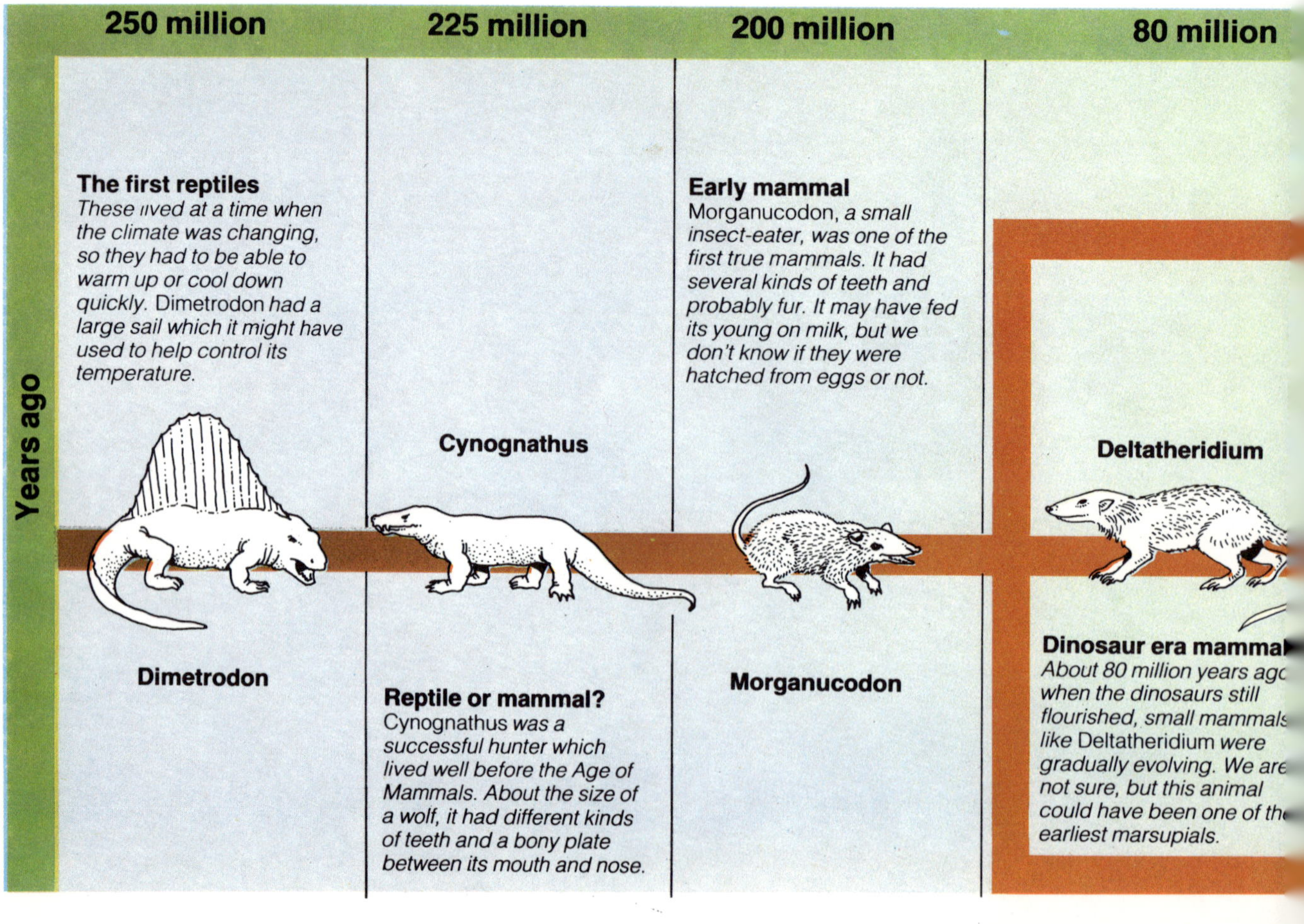

What is a mammal

Here is a typical mammal. It has fur, keeps warm and stays active, but to do this it needs lots of fuel (food) and a continuous supply of oxygen (from the air). The bony plate which separates the nose from the mouth means it can breathe and chew at the same time, for oxygen and food. Also it gives birth to babies, instead of laying eggs like a reptile. The babies are cared for and fed with milk by the mother. These and many other improvements over the reptiles meant that mammals could take over the world 65 million years ago.

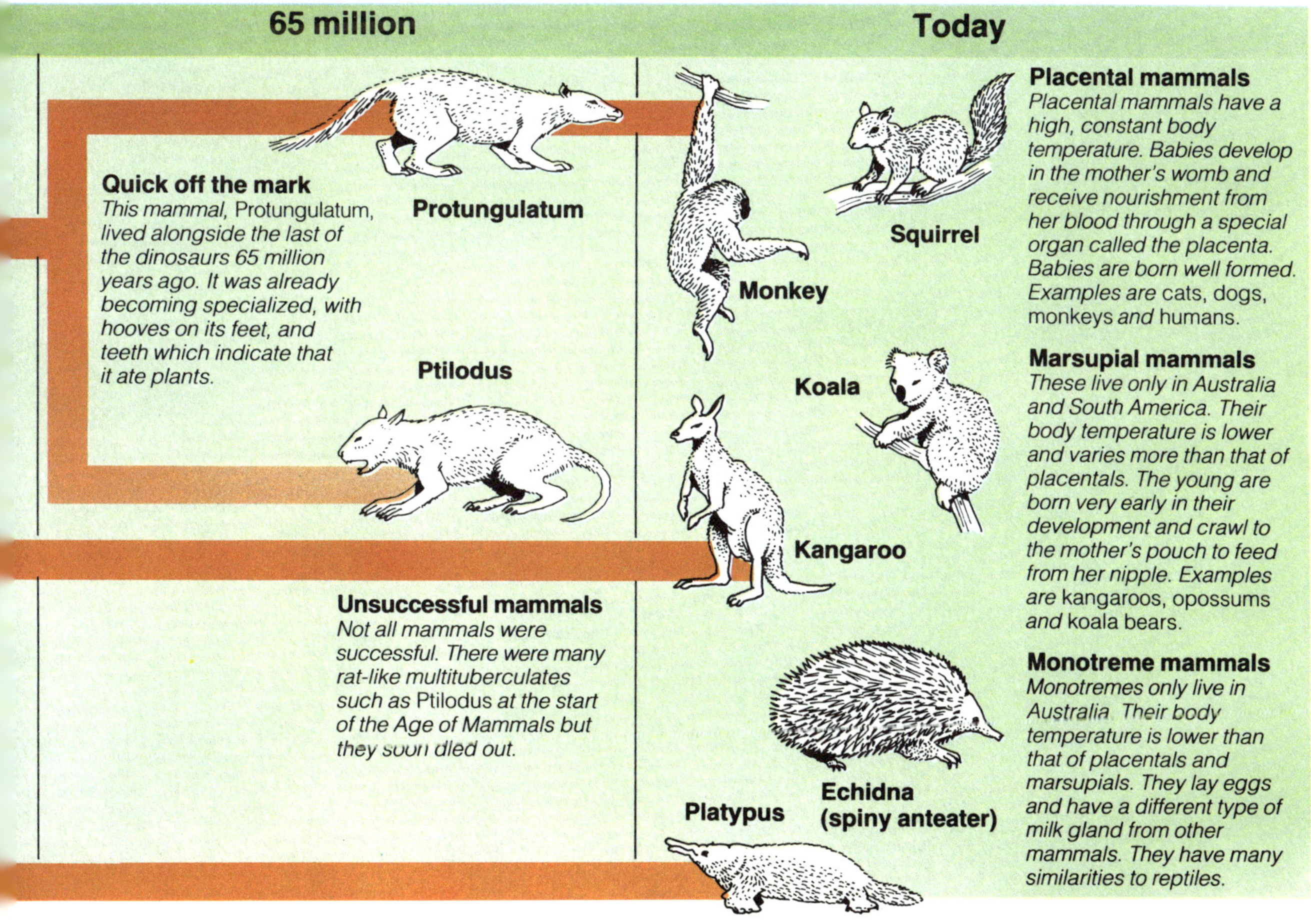

Quick off the mark
This mammal, Protungulatum, *lived alongside the last of the dinosaurs 65 million years ago. It was already becoming specialized, with hooves on its feet, and teeth which indicate that it ate plants.*

Unsuccessful mammals
Not all mammals were successful. There were many rat-like multituberculates such as Ptilodus *at the start of the Age of Mammals but they soon died out.*

Placental mammals
Placental mammals have a high, constant body temperature. Babies develop in the mother's womb and receive nourishment from her blood through a special organ called the placenta. Babies are born well formed. Examples are cats, dogs, monkeys *and* humans.

Marsupial mammals
These live only in Australia and South America. Their body temperature is lower and varies more than that of placentals. The young are born very early in their development and crawl to the mother's pouch to feed from her nipple. Examples are kangaroos, opossums *and* koala bears.

Monotreme mammals
Monotremes only live in Australia. Their body temperature is lower than that of placentals and marsupials. They lay eggs and have a different type of milk gland from other mammals. They have many similarities to reptiles.

Who was Cuvier?
Frenchman Georges Cuvier (1769 – 1832) was the first real palaeontologist (fossil expert). He had an amazing knowledge of living creatures, on which he based his fossil work. He was able to tell which fossil mammals were related to living ones, and deduce appearances from a single bone.

How do fossils form?

Most dead animals and plants are eaten or rot away, leaving no trace of their existence. Just occasionally, however, an animal dies and its body somehow ends up in a river or swamp, where it is soon covered by mud and buried. Even then the body may decay but, if conditions are right, the hard parts like bones and teeth will be preserved. For thousands or millions of years they stay there – until one day they are discovered by a lucky fossil-hunter. Fossils, then are the remains of long-dead animals and plants.

Hard parts such as bones and teeth may be unchanged when they are dug up, thousands of years after the animal has died. But usually chemical changes will have taken place, even though the size and shape of the original will have been preserved. Minerals seep in and harden the bone tissues, or water dissolves away the original material, replacing it with new minerals. Sometimes the bone is completely dissolved away, leaving only a hole in the rock. Later, this hole may be filled by a different material seeping into it, filling the place of the original remains. Rarely, a whole animal is preserved, trapped in amber or pickled in natural tar.

As well as the remains of actual animals, scientists have also discovered another type of fossil, called a trace fossil. This is a preserved trace or sign of an animal rather than the creature itself. Footprints, the marks where it rested or fed, or even fossil droppings are all trace fossils.

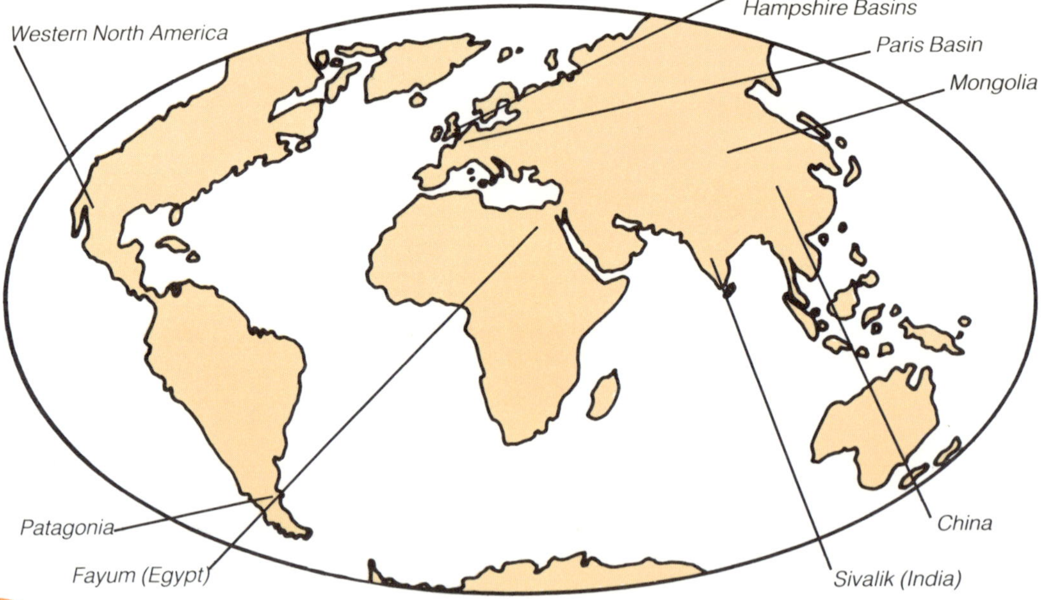

Where to look for fossils

Fossils are usually found in sedimentary rocks formed from the mud in lakes, rivers and seas. Look for fossil-bearing rocks in cliffs, riverbanks and road cuttings, but do be careful as these places can be dangerous. Remember, too, that you may need permission to visit quarries and cuttings.

The fossils described in this book nearly all come from fairly 'new' rocks – formed in the last 65 million years. If you go looking for fossils, you are more likely to find those of sea creatures such as shellfish, since mammal fossils are rare. Those embedded in rocks will have to be removed with a geological hammer. Try and split the rocks along natural breaks, or else you'll probably just destroy them.

The making of fossils

The animal leaves tracks and droppings as it walks along a riverbank.

It is attacked by another creature and its remains are washed into the river.

The footprints in the mud are baked dry, and covered by new mud. They can then be fossilized in the same way as the bones.

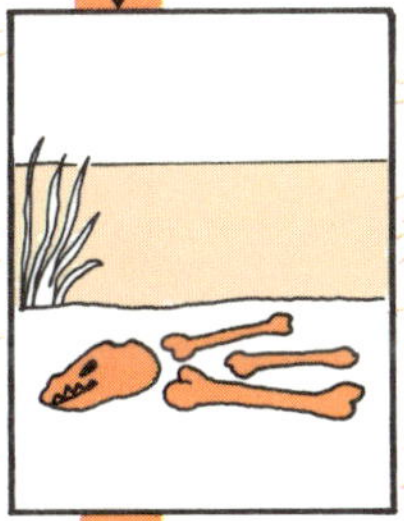

The soft parts rot away and the bones become stuck on the river bed.

Mud covers the bones and hardens into rock as more mud piles up on top.

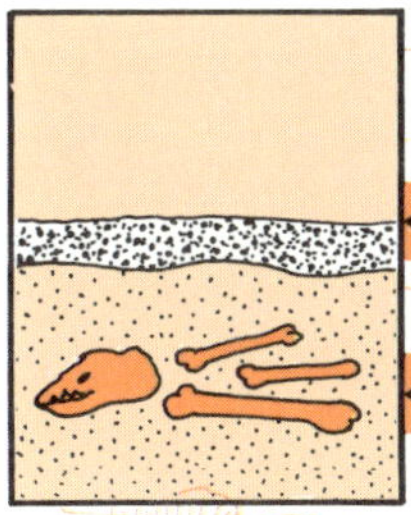

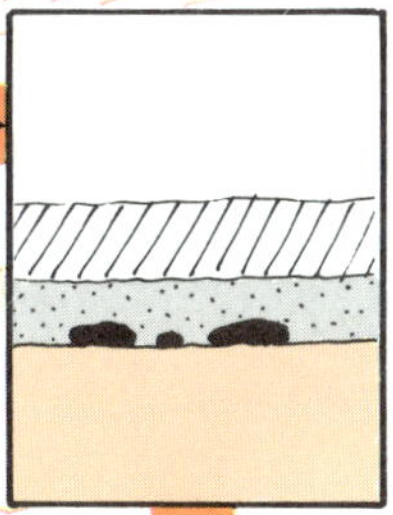

Over thousands and millions of years the land changes. More rocks are formed, wind and ice erode them away, volcanoes erupt, and earthquakes and other earth movements create new mountains or deep ravines. The prehistoric river bed may now be a desert or a mountain plateau.

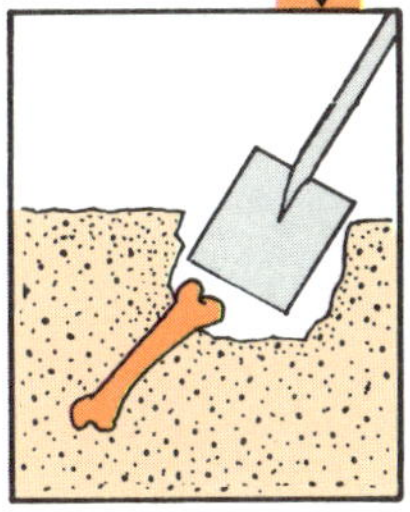

The bones may be dug up unchanged. These are called ***original remains.***

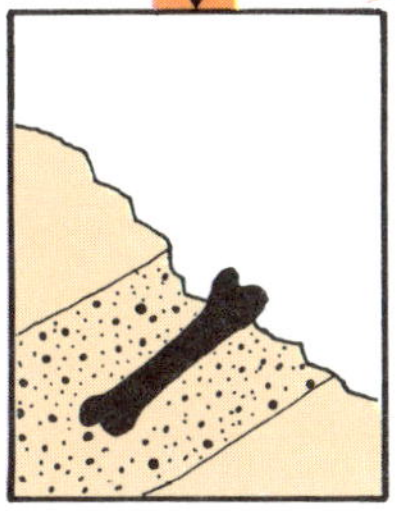

More usually, the bones will have been turned into stone by minerals in the rocks. These are called ***mineralized fossils.***

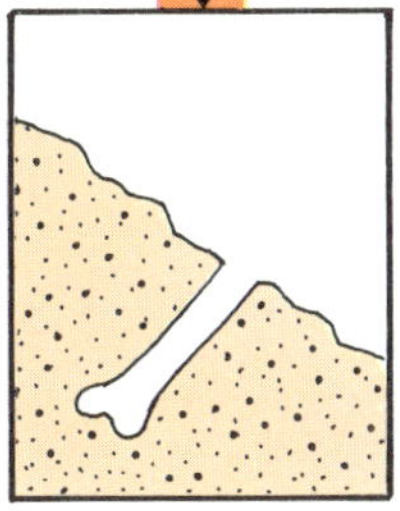

Some bones may have been completely dissolved away, leaving a hole in the rock the same shape as the bone. This is called a ***mould fossil.***

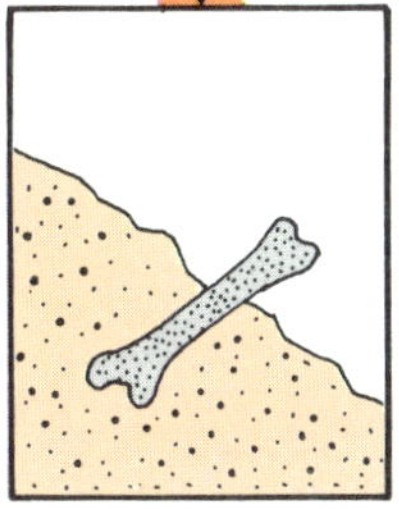

Sometimes new material seeps in and fills the mould, to form a replica of the bone. This is called a ***cast fossil.***

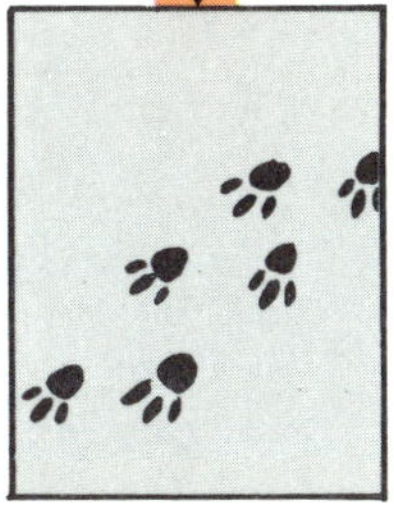

Excavation reveals fossil footprints and droppings. These are called ***trace fossils.***

Hard teeth

Mammal teeth are the likeliest fossils of these creatures to be found. They are the hardest parts and last longer than bones.

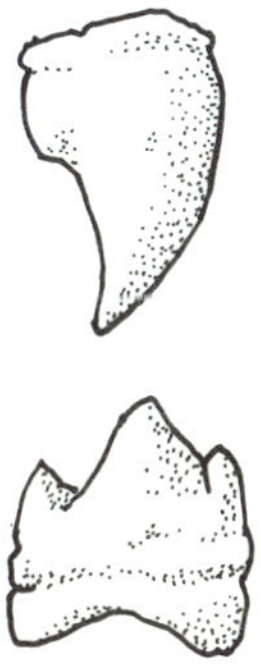

ALL SHAPES AND SIZES

Fifty million years ago, during the early Eocene period, the dinosaurs had all disappeared. But their place was quickly filled by mammals of all shapes and sizes. Birds, too, evolved rapidly. Giant flightless birds like *Diatryma* stalked the Earth, probably attacking and eating small mammals. But the birds soon lost the battle for supremacy on the ground, and mammals became the main land animals.

Although many mammals from 50 million years ago were quite different from those alive now, their surroundings were becoming increasingly like our own. The flowers and trees were similar to the varieties alive nowadays, and much of the Earth was forest. There were no wide, grassy plains, though, since grasses had not yet appeared.

Eocene fossils have given us clues which tell us that many parts of the world were much warmer than they are today. Warmth-loving fig trees and magnolias lived in Alaska. Crocodiles and turtles swam among palm trees in the swamps of southern England. And in most of Britain the climate was like Malaysia's is now.

Compared to modern mammals, many Eocene mammals look odd and clumsy. But we must remember that evolution works slowly, and that these animals were fairly new to their way of life. We can think of them as 'experimental' mammals which evolution was trying out in a world suddenly free of dinosaurs.

Protungulatum

Ectoconus

Weird and wonderful mammals

From 54 to 38 million years ago, during the Eocene period, the mammals developed rapidly. Those which had shared the Earth with the dinosaurs continued to survive and were joined by many new species. Before long a new set of weird and wonderful beasts had evolved to take advantage of the food and living spaces once used by the dinosaurs.

We have found out all this from the evidence of fossils. Many of the best Eocene fossils come from North America. Some more have been discovered in South America and Africa. The fossils tell us that some of the new mammal designs were very successful and existed for many millions of years. But other creatures came and went in a much shorter time. Some fossils show the remains of animals which have no equivalents today, making it difficult for us to imagine what they were like.

Quite early on in the Age of Mammals, all the main groups of mammals had appeared. These groups are called *orders*. During the Eocene there were 25 orders, perhaps more. Nowadays there are about 17 orders. So you can see that some of those early mammal 'designs' obviously didn't survive, while others gradually evolved into the mammals that live in the world today.

Early mammals

Some of the Eocene mammal groups were so early on in their development that it's difficult for palaeontologists to tell them apart. Many groups evolved from the same ancestors and looked very similar, even though their modern descendants are quite different. Early hoofed mammals like *Protungulatum* (top), which ate plants, looked very much like their hunting, meat-eating cousin *Ectoconus* (above). In the millions of years since then, these two groups have become more and more different, so that today they are represented by deer and tigers – much easier to tell apart!

North America in the early Eocene

1 Phenacodus *had tiny hoofs on its toes. Its short legs and weak teeth indicate that it probably ate only the softest leaves and shoots.*

2 Oxyaena *was an early kind of meat-eater called a* creodont. *It had sharp slicing teeth, flat feet and a small brain.*

3 Uintatherium *was the biggest mammal of its time, but has no present-day relatives. It browsed on tree leaves.*

4 Notharctus *was a very early kind of lemur, and may be an ancestor of modern lemurs.*

5 Diatryma *was a giant flightless bird. It could have used its sharp, strong beak for tearing apart other creatures, but some experts think that* Diatryma *was a vegetarian.*

Flippers and wings

During the Eocene, mammals became very specialized, some taking to the water, others to the air. The primitive whale *Basilosaurus* swam in the oceans, its legs having evolved into flippers. The first bats took to the skies, having developed wings of skin held out by the bones of their hands. And, like the bats of today, they had become specially adapted to hang upside-down when resting. In fact, bats have changed very little over the millions of years since they first appeared. Their design is much the same today as it was then.

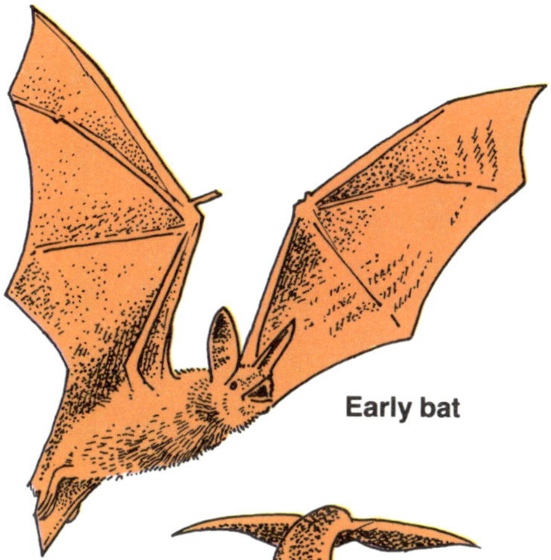

Early bat

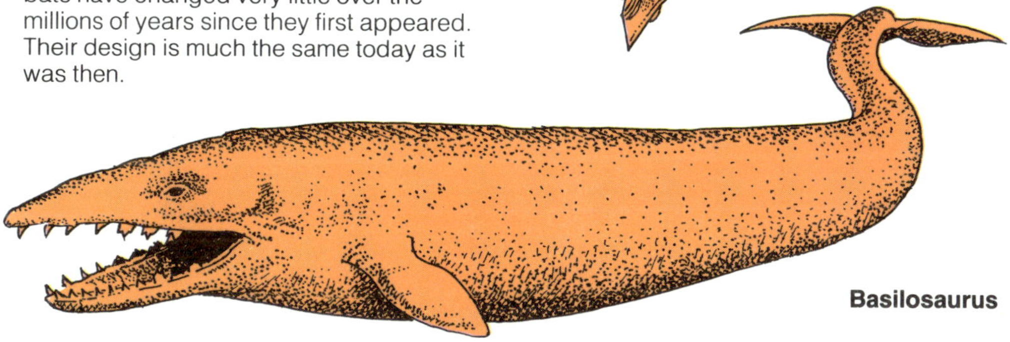

Basilosaurus

How to say...

Phenacodus
Fen-a-code-us

Oxyaena
Ox-eye-eena

Uintatherium
Winta-theer-ee-um

Notharctus
No-thark-tus

Diatryma
Die-a-try-ma

Andrewsarchus
Andrew-sark-us

Coryphodon
Korry-foe-don

Giants of the Eocene

Some Eocene mammals took over from the dinosaurs as the giants of the animal world. The rhino-like *Uintatherium* on page 12 was 2 metres tall and nearly 4 metres long – about the size of a Land-Rover!

In this panel you can see two more giants of the Eocene. *Andrewsarchus* has no living relatives, so the only clues we have to its way of life come from fossils. We can tell that it had rounded teeth and a heavy body – like a modern bear. So some experts think that it ate the same sort of food – almost anything! Others say it ate dead animals, thinking that it was similar to a hyaena. *Coryphodon* was one of the largest herbivores.

Coryphodon, *from Europe and North America, was a plant-eater 2.5 metres long.*

This fearsome beast is called Andrewsarchus, *and it lived in what is now Mongolia. Its skull alone was 1 metre long.*

Mammal meat-eaters

As more and more mammals came along they took to new ways of life. Some groups evolved to become plant-eaters, or *herbivores*, grazing in herds or browsing on the leaves of trees. It wasn't long before other mammals worked out that the herbivores themselves were a new source of food. So the meat-eaters, or *carnivores*, evolved.

Over millions of years the carnivores generally became bigger, so that they could tackle larger prey. They also developed large, sharp teeth so they could catch hold of and cut up their victims. Many carnivores that were a success during most of the Eocene belonged to one particular group – the *creodonts*.

The word creodont means 'flesh tooth'. The creodonts evolved from the small, insect-eating mammals like *Deltatheridium*, which were alive at the time of the last dinosaurs. During the Eocene, creodonts gradually became larger, and their teeth became bigger and sharper for dealing with meat. They developed big slicing, *carnassial*, teeth at the back of their mouths to act as shears for cutting tough skin and flesh.

Most creodonts had long, low heads with room for only a small, primitive brain. So they were probably not very clever. Many also had the old-fashioned type of mammal feet, where the sole and five toes were placed flat on the ground. A few stood up on their toes – a more advanced design for fast running.

As evolution continued the old-fashioned, slow and clumsy herbivores gradually disappeared or changed into quicker, cleverer versions. It is thought that the creodonts, which had a fairly primitive design and small brains, could not keep up with the changes. They gradually died out, and by 38 million years ago were nearly all extinct. Scientific evidence shows that modern meat-eaters actually evolved from a different mammal group called *fissipeds*.

Fight for food
Here a creodont lives up to its 'flesh tooth' name. A Tritemnodon *sets about making a meal of a* Notharctus.

Patriofelis

Oxyaenids

The oxyaenids were one of the two main groups of creodonts. They had short, squat skulls, short legs and flat feet which probably ended in blunt, rounded claws. *Oxyaena*, which gave its name to the group, was about the size of a badger but slimmer (see page 82). It could have killed animals up to the size of a rabbit, and possibly tried to catch larger prey. *Patriofelis*, shown here, was a medium-sized, cat-like creodont. *Megistotherium* was a giant creodont as big as a rhino. It was one of the few members of the creodont group to survive until the Miocene, 20 million years ago, and can be seen on page 97.

Hyaenodontids

This group of creodonts had long skulls and jaws and tended to stand on their toes. They were generally fairly small. *Hyaenodon* was one member of the group, and is shown on page 88. *Tritemnodon* (on the right) was another – a very slim, muscular animal which could probably outrun most other creatures of its time.

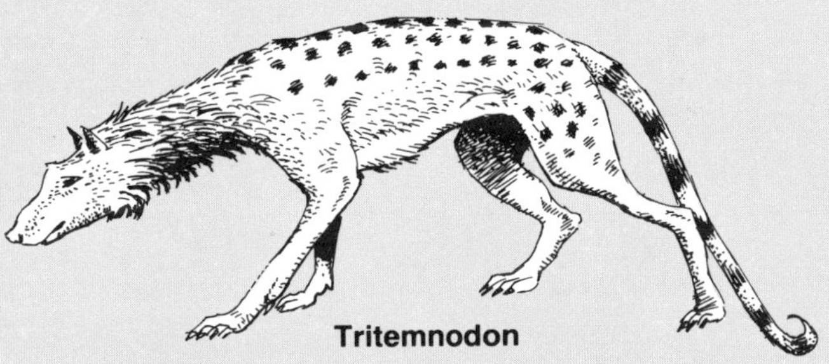

Tritemnodon

What is it?

Mesonyx was another primitive meat-eater. It was once thought to be the ancestor of modern carnivorous mammals, which are in the group called *Carnivora*. Then scientists changed their minds and put this creature into the creodont group. More recently opinions have changed again. Scientists now believe that *Mesonyx* was in fact a member of the condylarths, like *Andrewsarchus* on page 85. In another 20 years maybe things will have changed yet again...

Mesonyx

Truly a carnivore

Pseudocynodictis was one of the early fissipeds – the true carnivores that are the ancestors of today's cats, dogs, otters, weasels and many other meat-eaters. This slim, swift creature lived around 35 million years ago. It was the size of a large fox and probably led a fox-like way of life, hunting rabbits, rats, mice and other small creatures.

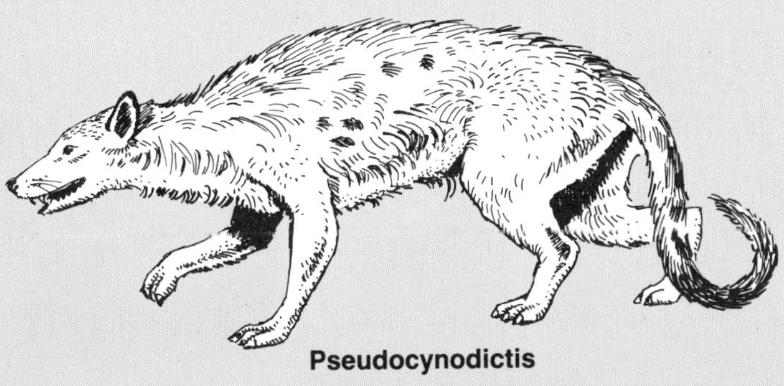

Pseudocynodictis

A TIME OF CHANGE

The Oligocene period, from 38 to 26 million years ago was a time of many changes. After the initial 'burst' of evolution early in the Age of Mammals, the groups were sorting themselves out. There were several surprisingly modern-looking types among the animals. The cats for example – those most specialized of meat-eaters – had developed rapidly, and were already very similar to the cats of today. They and other advancing groups were replacing the 'old-fashioned' mammals such as the creodonts.

Confusingly, some mammals looked like those alive now, but were not close relatives. *Archaeotherium* was like a large pig but it belonged to the entelodonts, a separate group from the one which gave rise to present-day pigs, giraffes, antelopes and other mammals with an even number of toes on each foot.

Other Oligocene animals were the ancestors of species around today, but they had not yet evolved into the typical shapes we would recognise. *Poebrotherium,* no bigger than a sheep, was a small, early type of camel that already had just two toes on each foot – like today's camels.

Some Oligocene creatures – like *Merycoidodon,* which looked like a cross between a pig and a sheep – were very successful at the time, but died out. The Oligocene was an interesting phase in mammal evolution, and it presents palaeontologists with plenty of puzzles.

Horses, rhinos and tapirs

The great Oligocene success story involved the group of mammals which are called 'perissodactyl ungulates' – hoofed mammals with an odd number of toes on each foot. These are the horses, rhinos and tapirs. During the Oligocene they flourished in a way that has never been seen before or since.

When we gather together all the fossils of a certain group, such as horses or rhinos, it is tempting to arrange them in an 'evolutionary tree'. We may expect the tree to be nice and neat, with just a few tidy branches. We imagine one species evolving into another, which is the ancestor of the next, and so on, in a line up to the present day.

Unfortunately, nature is rarely so straightforward. The simple 'tree' is in reality a complicated, twiggy bush. The fossils we find are only the tips of a few twigs; the rest is guesswork based on the evidence discovered. And even though we can place animals in an 'evolutionary line', like the rhinos shown opposite, this does not mean that each creature in the line is the ancestor of the one after it. Sometimes they may be. In other cases they probably aren't. We can never know for sure. If someone digs up a completely new kind of fossil the experts may have to draw up the evolutionary trees all over again.

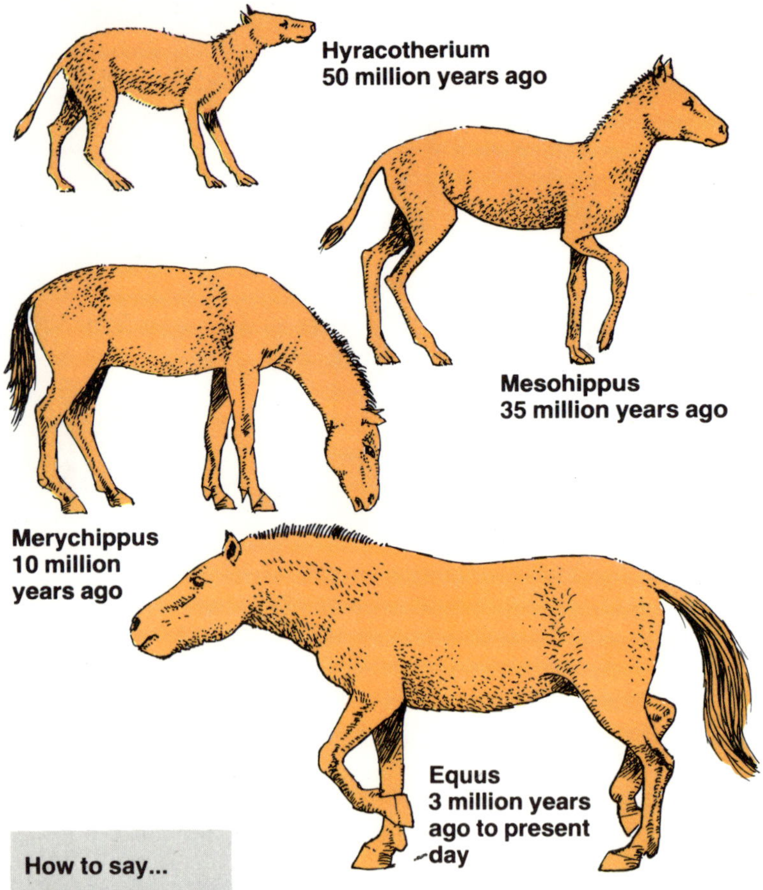

How the horse evolved

50 million years ago, the first horse-like creatures lived in Eocene forests. They were only just bigger than a domestic cat, with five tiny nails on each foot.

Fossils through the ages show that members of the horse group gradually became bigger, with longer and thinner legs. The number of toes on each foot was five, then three, and today it's one – the horse's hoof. The teeth and jaws became bigger and better at dealing with tough foods such as grass. Today the wild horse is a fast-moving, plains-dwelling, herd-living creature.

How to say...

Hoplophoneus
Hop-low-fon-ee-us

Archaeotherium
Ark-ee-owe-theer-ee-um

Poebrotherium
Poe-ee-bro-theer-ee-um

Merycoidodon
Merry-coy-doe-don

Hyaenodon
High-een-owe-don

Nightfall at an American river during the Oligocene

1 Hoplophoneus *was an early sabre-toothed cat. Its long canine teeth were used to stab and kill its prey.*

2 Archaeotherium *had tusk-like canine teeth. Fossilized examples suggest that it may have used them to dig and grub up roots.*

3 Poebrotherium *was a very early kind of camel. It was only 50 cms tall at the shoulder.*

4 Merycoidodon *has no descendants living today. Its teeth show it to be related to cud-chewers like cows.*

5 Hyaenodon *was a meat-eating creodont. It was large and heavily built, like today's wolves.*

6 *Prehistoric bats flitted over the dark river, searching for flies and other insects. Bats had already been around for millions of years.*

Rhinos through the ages

Rhinos developed from an early tapir-like animal and the prehistoric ones came in all shapes and sizes. Some didn't have horns, others had one or more. Of the dozens which have lived in the past, there are only five species left alive today They are all rare, partly because they are hunted by humans. It would be terrible if we were responsible for making them extinct, so finishing the 'rhino tree' for ever.

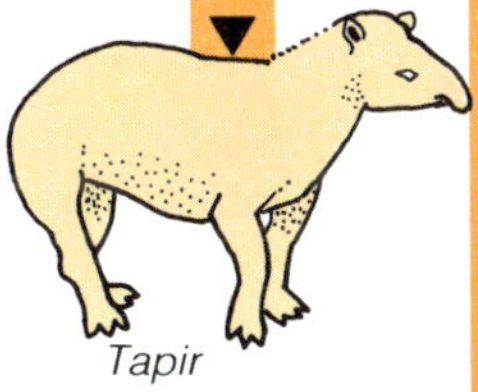

Mainstream rhinos

The main 'branch' of rhino evolution started with animals like *Caenopus*, which was about 2.4 metres long. It had three toes on each foot, large front teeth, but no horn. For millions of years rhinos were like this – heavy bodied, browsing, thick-skinned creatures. One, *Diceratherium*, had two horns.

Giant hornless rhinos

One side-line from the main branch of rhino evolution were giant hornless rhinos – like *Paraceratherium*.

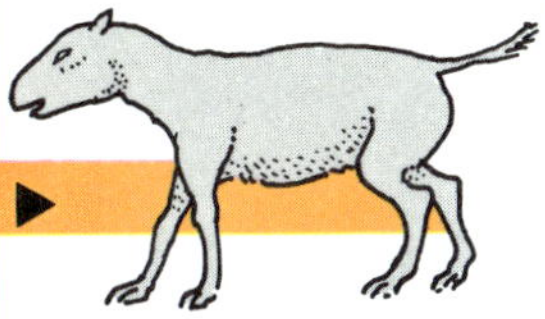

Running rhinos

One rhino group became more horse-like and able to run swiftly. The running rhino *Hyracodon* was about 75 cms tall, lightly built, with long legs and three hoofed toes on each foot. Like many primitive rhinos, it had no horn.

Wallowing rhinos

The wallowing rhinos were an offshoot from the running rhinos. *Metamynodon* was rather typical of this group – rather tubby and short-legged. We think that they swam and wallowed in water, much like hippos do today.

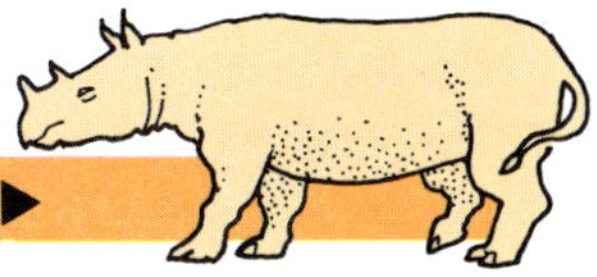

Today's rhinos

There are only five species of rhino alive today. These are the *Sumatran, Indian, Javan* and the *African black* and *white* rhinos.

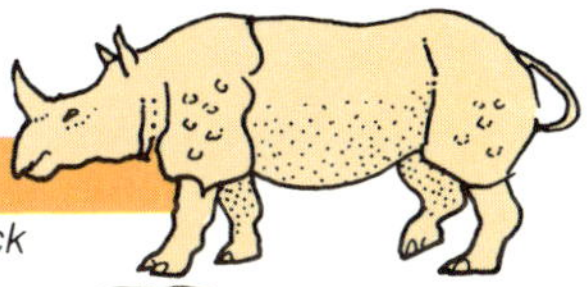

Woolly rhinos

During the Ice Age, some rhinos developed long, thick coats to keep out the cold. They became extinct only a few thousand years ago.

Grazing rhinos

A few of the later rhinos specialized in grazing. They included *Elasmotherium,* which had very strong grinding teeth. This was the largest of the horned rhinos, with a huge horn 2 metres long on a strong skull 1 metre long.

A giant among giants

The biggest mammal that ever lived on land was a giant hornless rhino from 30 million years ago. Its name was *Paraceratherium* and you can see it in the picture below. These giants evolved in Asia during the Oligocene and survived for millions of years. Opposite, you can see two more giants that lived at the same time.

Paraceratherium was a vast animal, over twice the size of today's elephants. It stood 5.5 metres high at the shoulder, was over 8 metres long, and must have weighed around 17 tonnes. It had a long neck but a small head for its size. Even so, when it stretched up, the end of its snout could have been 7 metres or more above the ground – easily high enough to reach on to the roof of an ordinary house.

This giant's skull was 1.3 metres long, rather low, with a curious dome in the middle. The front teeth were small tusk-like cones. Behind them in the jaw was a gap, then came the cheek teeth (premolars and molars) which were flat and adapted to crushing leaves. The lack of bone at the front of the skull suggests that the upper lip was long and grasping, maybe like that of today's African black rhino.

Paraceratherium needed strong pillar-like legs to support its weight, but these were by no means fat and clumsy. In fact, this giant was probably quite nimble despite its huge size.

Sprightly giants
Although large, Paraceratherium *was probably very agile. Here a herd of these creatures browse on bushes and trees, grasping the leaves with their pointed lips.*

Double horned giants

On the right you can see two more giants from the Oligocene. *Arsinoitherium* lived in Africa. It was a clumsy plant-eater 3.4 metres long and had huge double horns on its head. It is likely that it used its horns for self-defence and perhaps in battles over territories and mates.

Brontotherium was one of the biggest titanotheres, measuring over 2.5 metres at the shoulder. These creatures were descended from the same group as horses. As the 'titan' part of their name suggests, many were very large, and were common in many parts of the world some 35 million years ago. No-one has been able to decide why *Brontotherium* had such a large bony double-horn, but one theory is that it developed as a result of *allometry*. This is when one part of a creature's body develops at a different rate from the rest.

For instance, over a few million years an animal's body might become twice the size of its ancestors – but its horn could grow to four times as big. This process of allometry has happened in many different animal groups, but we are not sure how it occurs. The illustrations below show how we imagine it may have happened in *Brontotherium*.

Arsinoitherium

Brontotherium

1 *Ancestor of* Brontotherium, *with small body and horn.*

2 Brontotherium, *with large body and very large horn.*

3 *Suppose* Brontotherium *had lived on and evolved for a few more million years. Its horns would have continued to grow at a much faster rate than its body...then they would have been absolutely gigantic!*

LIFE ON THE PLAINS

The animals that live in our modern world are greatly affected by the plants growing in their environment. This was also true during prehistoric times. During the long period called the Miocene, which was from 26 to 7 million years ago, grasses became important plants. This was because the climate in many parts of the world became drier, so the drought-resistant grasslands spread as the rain-loving forests died back.

As the plants changed, so did the animals. Shady forest glades with their succulent leaves, shoots and fruits gave way to open plains of tough grass, which needed equally tough teeth to make use of it. It was a case of 'browsers out, grazers in'. Many of the old-style browsing mammals became less common and new types, grazing on the grasses and other ground-growing plants, took over.

At the start of the Miocene there were still many types of rhino, but the other main group of odd-toed hoofed mammals, the horses, became much more widespread. The even-toed hoofed mammals also became numerous, many of them living in herds.

By the end of the period plains-dwelling herbivores such as antelopes were in existence, along with deer and giraffes. A new selection of carnivores evolved to prey on these new plant-eaters. The world was changing, and the mammals, ever adaptable, were changing with it.

How to say...

Syndyoceras
Sin-dee-owe-sare-us

Alticamelus
Alt-ee-camel-us

Diceratherium
Die-sare-a-theer-ee-um

Daphoenodon
Daff-een-owe-don

Moropus
Morrow-puss

Lifestyles of long ago

The idea that certain parts of a living thing develop to carry out a particular task is a cornerstone of evolutionary thinking. In other words, the job shapes the part. We can see this as we look at today's animals and the food they eat: the long neck of the giraffe, the trunk of the elephant, the claws of the cat, and so on.

This way of thinking can be used with fossils. For example, we can guess at the type of food eaten by a prehistoric mammal by looking at its fossil teeth and skull. Does it have the flat, grinding teeth of a plant-eater or the sharp, pointed ones of a carnivore? We can also be more confident about our deductions by making comparisons with present-day animals.

The general size and shape of a fossil mammal can tell us much about its lifestyle. For instance, a bulky creature weighing several tonnes, like the

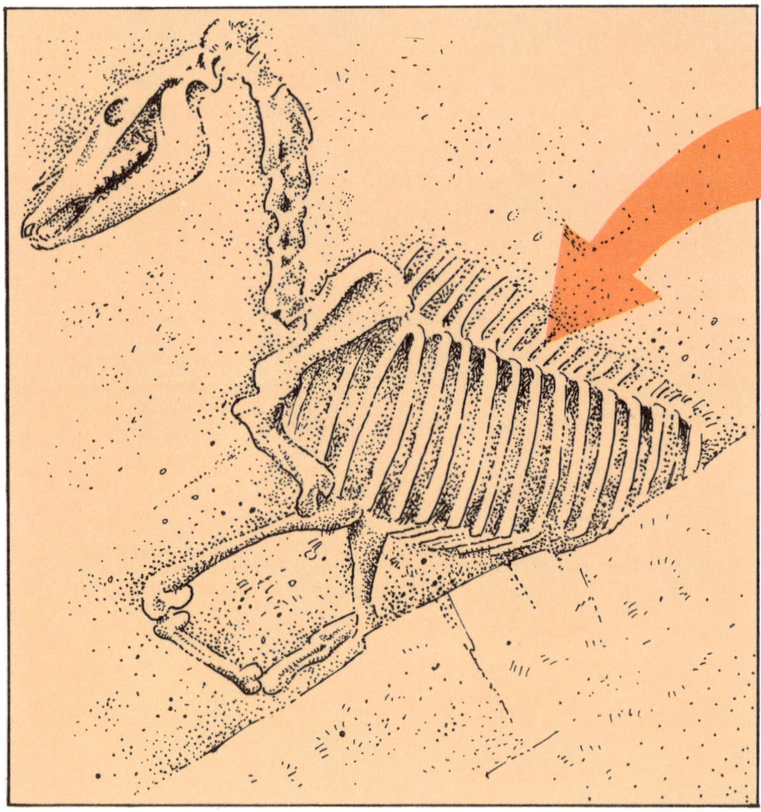

Plant remains

Herds, families and food

Present-day hoofed mammals often live in herds. Finding fossils of ancient mammals in groups leads us to suspect that they also lived in herds, and that they all died together in a flood or similar disaster. If the bones are of just a few adults and youngsters, then the group was probably a family party, rather than a herd of adults with only a few young.

Further aspects of an animal's lifestyle may be guessed from other remains found with or near its fossils. Plant remains, like those shown above, are sometimes found – leaves, seeds or wood from forest trees, or grasses from plains and prairies. If an animal's fossils are always associated with remains of a certain type of plant, then we can guess that the animal probably lived in that sort of habitat.

North American prairie during the Miocene

1 Syndyoceras *was an even-toed hoofed mammal. Although rather like an antelope in appearance it belonged to a more primitive group.*

2 Alticamelus *was an early type of camel – probably without a hump. It was 3.5 metres tall.*

3 Diceratherium *was a two-horned rhino, one of the 'mainstream' rhinos described on page 91.*

4 Daphoenodon *was an early dog of the group sometimes called bear-dogs. It was 1.4 metres long with a heavy build and short legs. It probably ate some plant food as well as meat.*

5 Moropus *was an odd mammal related to horses and rhinos, but it had claws on its front feet. As you can read on page 98, we are not at all sure about its way of life.*

Diceratherium on the previous spread, could never have climbed trees. Nor could a long, thin-legged hoofed mammal like *Syndyoceras*. Instead, we can tell from its skeleton that *Syndyoceras* was a runner. This 'running leg' design can be seen over and over again, from the fleet-footed dinosaurs to the horses of today. The legs are long, slim and easy to swing. The strong, leg-moving muscles are concentrated at the top, near the body, while the lower part of the leg is very light, with a long foot and as few toes as possible. This design increases stiffness for a good push-off against the ground, and decreases the number of bones and joints – and so the weight – at the leg's tip. The lighter the lower leg and foot are, the easier and faster they can be swung when running.

We often find fossils of one creature with, or near another. If this happens many times, it's unlikely to be coincidence. Then we can make intelligent guesses about why the fossils are together. For example, fossils of the giant North African creodont *Megistotherium* are often found with the fossilized bones of primitive elephants called mastodons. So we can deduce from this that mastodons were a favourite prey of the huge *Megistotherium*.

Well-suited killer
Megistotherium *had huge canine teeth and large attachments for strong muscles to close its jaws. It weighed over 900 kgs, which makes it the largest flesh-eating mammal known! Here it is attacking a mastodon.*

Mammal puzzles

Some mammals from the past are very similar to the mammals of today. Using today's species as examples, we can make good guesses about the prehistoric mammals' way of life. But there are some fossils with no living equivalents, and no close relatives. Several fossils have such an odd appearance or such an unusual combination of features that it is very difficult to guess how they lived, and the scientists argue about them. They may have different ideas about what the animal looked like and how it lived. This is why you may find quite varied pictures of the same animal in different books.

Moropus ('awkward feet') belonged to the group known as chalicotheres, and is one of the most puzzling cases. *Moropus* lived during the Miocene and was a distant relative of horses and rhinos. Yet it looks like a 'misfit' mammal, made up of spare parts. It had a horse-like head and teeth; its body was massive and heavy; its front legs were longer than its back legs; and its feet had claws rather than hoofs, the front claws being especially large.

Moropus has been reconstructed in several different ways, as you can see here and on page 94. Some experts now believe that it may have shambled along on its front knuckles, rather like a chimpanzee. Its teeth show it to be a herbivore, which leads us to ask what it used its claws for. Did it dig up roots, pull leafy branches to its mouth, or defend itself with them? It's certainly hard for us to tell with such a confusing creature that looks like a cross between a horse, a bear and an ape.

'Spare parts' mammal

The 'spare parts' mammal, *Moropus*, has been constructed from fossils in many ways – as you can read about opposite. Here we see it in what scientists now believe is the most likely form.

Stabbers or slashers?

Sabre-toothed cats have had a long and varied history, but we can only imagine what they used their long, curving teeth for. These weapons were so long that they could not have snapped shut on prey, in the way that those of modern cats do, and were too delicate to risk stabbing prey with. Instead they may have been used to cut and slash at the victims' neck, so that the main blood vessels were severed. Some people have even suggested that sabre-toothed cats fed only on the blood of their prey, pointing out that the very small teeth in the rest of the cat's jaw would have been useless for crunching up gristle or bone.

Macrauchenia is another fossil mammal that has caused many arguments. It used to live in South America and its skeleton shows that it had nostril holes high up on its skull. But scientists have developed three different ideas about *why* they were there.

Some say *Macrauchenia* lived in swamps and that it could submerge itself to escape from danger, leaving just its nostrils above the surface of the water so it could breathe.

Then again, *Macrauchenia* could have had a small trunk for gathering food. But its skull is neater around the nostril holes than those of modern trunked mammals, like elephants and tapirs.

The last and most likely suggestion is that its nostrils could have been closed by muscular flaps to keep out dust and sand – like those of modern camels. If this is true, then this clue leads us to deduce that *Macrauchenia* lived on the sandy plains.

Macrauchenia
Three 'incarnations' of the mammal Macrauchenia:
1 *The swamp creature.*
2 *The elephant look-alike.*
3 *The plains dweller.*

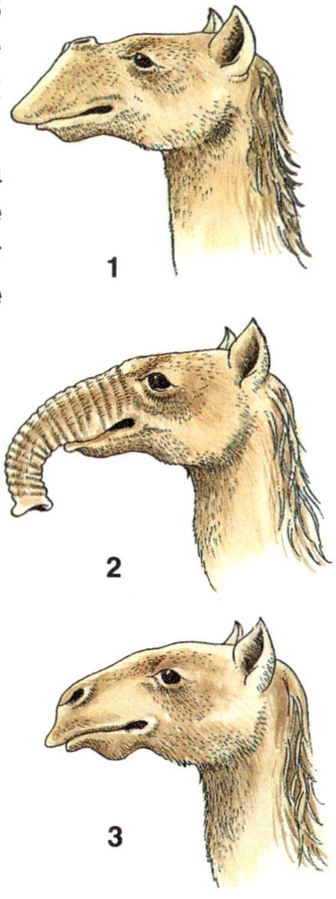

MAMMALS OF YESTERYEAR

In the Pliocene period, from 7 to 2 million years ago, the mammals of the world were mostly similar to today's. Deer, pigs, giraffes and many antelope species roamed over Europe, Asia, and probably Africa. They were almost identical to today's versions. In fact in Europe, Asia and North America, more than three-quarters of the mammals belonged to groups still in existence now, although some of the individual species were different.

Yet in some parts of the world, such as South America and Australia, strange, old-fashioned mammals still survived. And we don't have to look far for the reason. These two continents had been isolated from the rest of the world by stretches of ocean for millions of years. Their mammals had evolved in isolation, developing their own particular mixtures of species.

There were still many primitive *marsupial* (pouched) mammals on these two 'island' continents, even though they had long since died out in other parts of the world. Some marsupials, such as the sabre-toothed cat *Thylacosmilus*, had developed astonishing similarities to more advanced mammals elsewhere, because they had similar ways of life. Others were quite unique. Today there are still many marsupial species in Australia, and some in South America, but they are under great threat from the more advanced *placental* mammals – including the most 'advanced' of all, the human.

How to say...

Thylacosmilus
Thigh-la-cos-mile-us

Toxodon
Tox-owe-don

Glyptodon
Glipp-tow-don

Macrauchenia
Mack-roar-keen-ee-a

Trunks and tusks

For most of the last 35 million years there have been mammals that coud be loosely described as 'elephants'. The steps in elephant evolution are quite complex, so it is difficult to draw up their family tree. What is clear, though, is that in the past there have been many, many elephant types of all shapes and sizes. You can see some of them on the opposite page. The two species alive today, the African and Indian elephants, are a small reminder of a once numerous and widespread group.

Elephant evolution is sometimes traced back to a small pig-like creature called *Moeritherium* that lived 50 million years ago. But, although this shows us what the elephants' ancestors may have looked like, we cannot be sure it actually *was* their relation.

Palaeomastodon and *Phiomia*, which lived about 35 million years ago, are the first mammals we can confidently include in the elephant group, which is called the *Proboscidea*. These were large mammals with short trunks and tusks. After them, the main story of elephant evolution has been one of increasing body size – perhaps because this made them less vulnerable to enemies. The head and jaws also changed and became shorter, possibly because really big jaws were too heavy and awkward. As the jaws became shorter, the upper lip and nose became longer to form the trunk which could reach for and grip food.

To feed their large bodies, elephants also developed better teeth for grinding large quantities of plants and for coping with tough grasses. Today's elephants have huge molar teeth covered with many ridges. And to help them even further, they have three sets of these molars which appear one after the other during the animal's life. The third and last set of molars come into use when the elephant is about 30 years old, and as these teeth wear away the elephant's long life draws to a close...

Distant relations?
Moeritherium, *above, is sometimes said to be an ancestor of the elephants, but we cannot really be sure that this is so. The deinotheres (one of which is shown on the right) look a lot more like elephants, but are suspected to have evolved separately. You would have to go a long way back into the Age of Mammals to find a common ancestor.*

South America during the Pliocene

1 Thylacosmilus *was a fierce meat-eating marsupial. It had long upper canine teeth (sabre teeth), with deep flaps sticking out from the lower jaw to support and protect them.*

2 Toxodon *was one of the last of the primitive hoofed mammals to live in South America. The size of a rhino, with stumpy legs, it has been described by some scientists as a 'gigantic guinea pig'.*

3 Glyptodon *was an armadillo-like creature, up to 3 metres long, which was well protected by interlocking bony plates in its skin. Its large, strong molar teeth suggest that it ate grasses and other plants.*

4 Macrauchenia *belonged to the group of hoofed mammals called litopterns. This species was camel-like in appearance and possibly had the same habits.*

Elephant ancestors

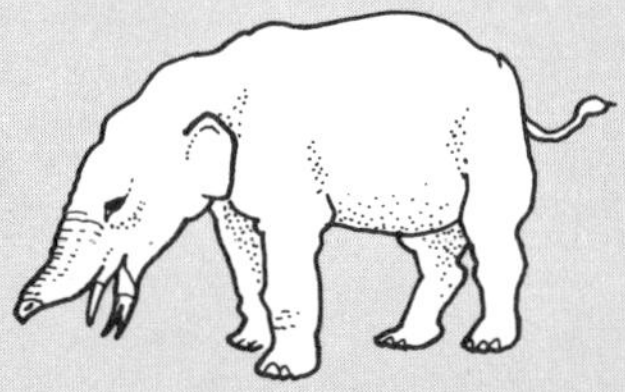

Palaeomastodon from 35 million years ago was about 2 metres long. It had four long, shovel-like tusks in its jaw. The teeth were rather pig-like, showing that it ate soft vegetation.

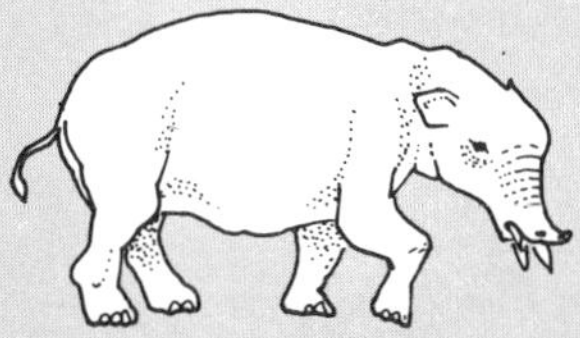

Phiomia also from about 35 million years ago, was 1.2 metres long. The shape of its fossil skull in the nose and upper-jaw area suggests the beginnings of the elephant trunk.

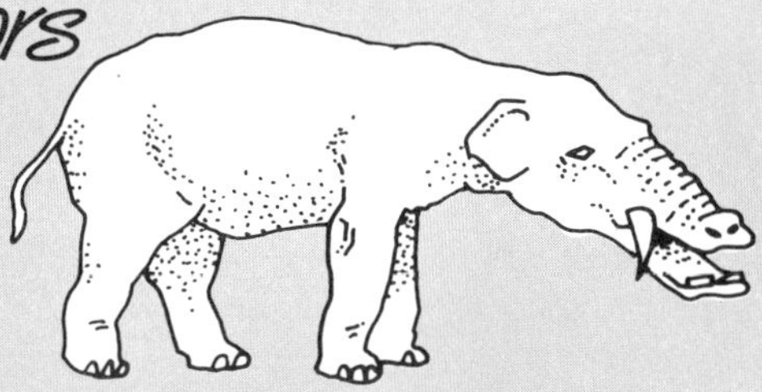

Platybelodon was around 2 metres tall, and lived from 20 million years ago. It had short upper tusks and blade-like lower tusks. Its jaws and mouth worked like a shovel to dig plants out of the ground.

Gomphotherium lived about 15 to 20 million years ago. It was about 1.5 metres tall and had four tusks.

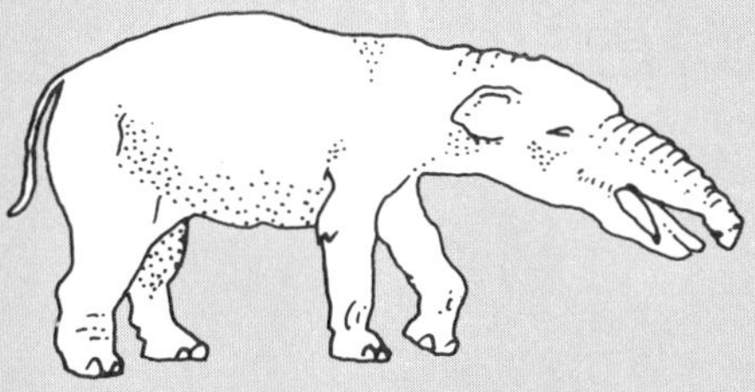

Amebelodon lived around 5 million years ago. It stood 2 metres at the shoulder, and used its elongated 'lips' to shovel food into its mouth.

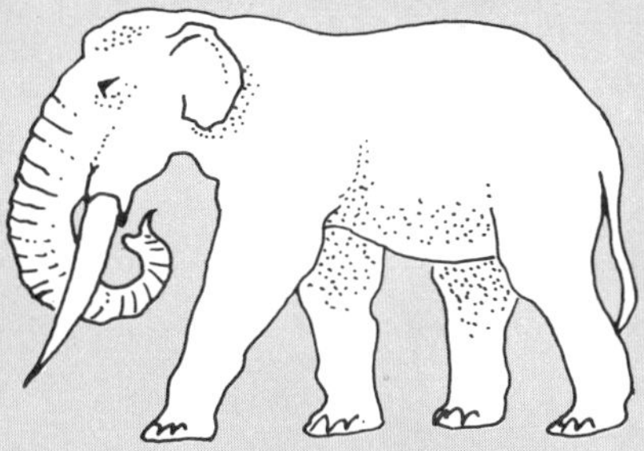

Palaeoloxodon was big even for an elephant, standing 4.3 metres at the shoulder, with an overall height of perhaps 5 metres. It lived in forests and only died out about 250,000 years ago.

Mammoths were elephants that flourished on the Earth 2 million years ago. Some lived in warm climates, but when the Ice Ages came only the famous woolly mammoths could survive the cold. They developed the most ridged teeth of all elephants, presumably because of the tough, strong plants which grew in the cold conditions. Woolly mammoths were about 4.5 metres tall and, unlike all other elephants (as far as we know), they were covered in long hair for warmth. We know this because woolly mammoths have been found frozen solid in the ice of Siberia, perfectly preserved.

Dwarf elephants evolved on some islands, especially in the Mediterranean. They were similar to *Palaeoloxodon* but only 1 metre high.

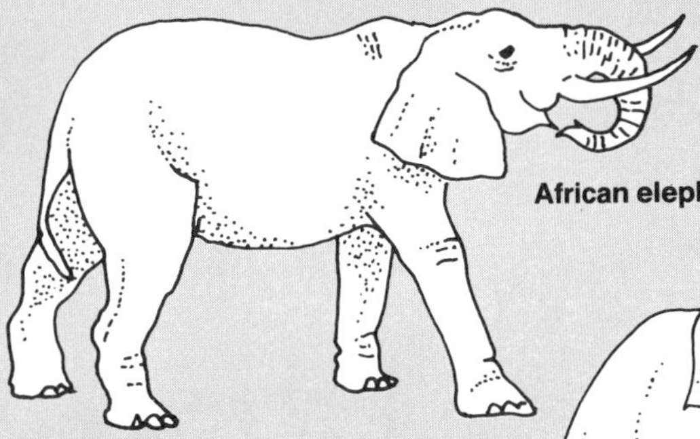

African elephant

Indian elephant

Today's African and **Indian** elephants are the only species that still exist. The African elephant is 3.5 metres tall at the shoulder, perhaps more, and has much larger ears than the Indian version.

The dawn of Darwin's Ideas

Darwin's voyage
Darwin travelled to South America and the Pacific on a ship called the Beagle. *The map on the right shows its passage around South America and the Galapagos Islands.*

On the shores of Patagonia, Darwin found many fossils, as you can see in the picture below. He dug up the fossilized bones of lots of extinct animals and study of these led him to form his theories about evolution.

Nowadays nearly all palaeontologists accept the general idea of evolution. We almost take it for granted that animals and plants gradually change with time, as one generation follows another. Sometimes a particular kind of animal becomes extinct or changes into a completely new and different species.

One of the main reasons we believe in the idea of evolution is that we can imagine how it happens. As the world slowly changes, it suits some animals better than others. These well-adapted types thrive, while others die out. We call this 'the survival of the fittest', and we owe the idea to the naturalist Charles Darwin.

In 1831 Darwin sailed round the world on a ship called the *Beagle*, which spent five years mapping the coasts of South America. The things that Darwin saw convinced him of the theory of evolution, even though people laughed at his ideas. He visited the Galapagos Islands, where he saw a variety of closely-related living species, and spent time in South America where he found many wonderful and unique mammal fossils. These were the most important parts of his voyage.

Darwin saw at first hand just what odd and gigantic animals had lived in the area called Patagonia, and this set him thinking about how and why animals became extinct. He also studied the

Giant ground sloths

Darwin's finds included several gigantic ground sloths. Big as elephants, they are thought to have rested on their heavy back legs and pulled leaves and twigs to their mouths with their long-clawed hands and long tongues. *Megatherium* (right) was the biggest of all, at 6 metres long. Ground sloths survived in South America for over 30 million years, dying out only a few thousand years ago. Sometimes their 'mummified' (dried out) remains are found in caves, along with their droppings, which show what they ate. The only sloths still living in South America today are the small, climbing tree sloths.

rocks and saw for himself clear evidence that the sea levels had changed, how rock layers had formed, and how fossils differed in various layers.

The reason for the uniqueness of the South American mammals is that for most of the Age of Mammals, South America was an island. Before the Age of Mammals all the continents had been joined together. But they split up and drifted apart and, early in mammal history, South America became separated from the rest.

The animals living in South America evolved along their own lines. The *marsupials*, under threat in other parts, did very well. But by 2 million years ago South America had drifted to its present position, joined to North America by the narrow Isthmus of Panama. In the struggles that followed, the South American animals generally came off worse. Big meat-eating marsupials such as *Thylacosmilus* (see pages 100-101) were replaced by cats, dogs and otters. Horses, guanacos and deers took over from the primitive hoofed mammals. A few animals like the opossum and the armadillo travelled north and still live in North America. But generally the northerners took over and animals from the south became extinct.

Charles Darwin took many years to work on his evidence about the survival of the fittest. He saw Nature as selecting those best fitted to the surroundings. Another naturalist, Alfred Wallace, also thought of this. In 1858 Darwin and Wallace wrote a scientific paper together. Then in 1859 Darwin published his book: *On the Origin of Species by Means of Natural Selection* (which is often called simply *The Origin of Species*). This became one of the most influential books ever published.

Charles Darwin
Darwin (1809-82) was only 22 years old when he joined the Beagle's *voyage as naturalist. His pioneering work has made the theory of evolution almost universally accepted.*

New mammals for old

Even though we may not know all the details, the general trends in evolution, between the mammals of 50 or 60 million years ago and those of today, are fairly clear.

For example, the early plant-eaters such as *Coryphodon* and *Uintatherium* were heavily built, clumsy and had small brains. They were sitting suppers for the better carnivores of their day. Compare them to a modern horse or gazelle with its light build, speed, keen senses of sight, hearing and smell, and its relatively large brain. It is easy to see how improvements like this helped in escaping from predators. But as the plant-eaters changed, so did the meat-eaters – they had to, or they would have died out.

There are, however, many evolutionary puzzles. Opossums have scarcely altered for 60 million years. Pangolins (scaly anteaters) and bats have remained almost the same for 50 million years or more. Why? Is it that evolution quickly came up with a 'first-time hit', a creature so perfectly in tune with its way of life that no more improvements were possible? Or is it just their good fortune that no other animals have evolved to knock them from their positions?

At the other end of the scale we know of mammal groups that have never stopped changing. Their fossils show that one type evolved into another, and so on up to the present day. The even-toed hoofed mammals make up a group that has evolved like this. They existed in many different forms 30 million years ago, developing into the huge variety of antelopes and others that wander the African plains today. What's the secret of their success?

Well, we must admit that there are no good answers to these questions at the moment, but there are plenty of theories. Perhaps a new Charles Darwin will come along to pick up the clues and discover more of the secrets of the past.

Even-toed hoofed mammals

There are so many species of even-toed fossil mammals that it is difficult to keep track of them all. The oreodonts such as *Merycoidodon* (left) and cainotheres like *Dichobune* (above) were early members of the group. Nowadays, the same group contains dozens of species – of pigs, hippos, camels, sheep, deer, oxen and many, many antelopes.

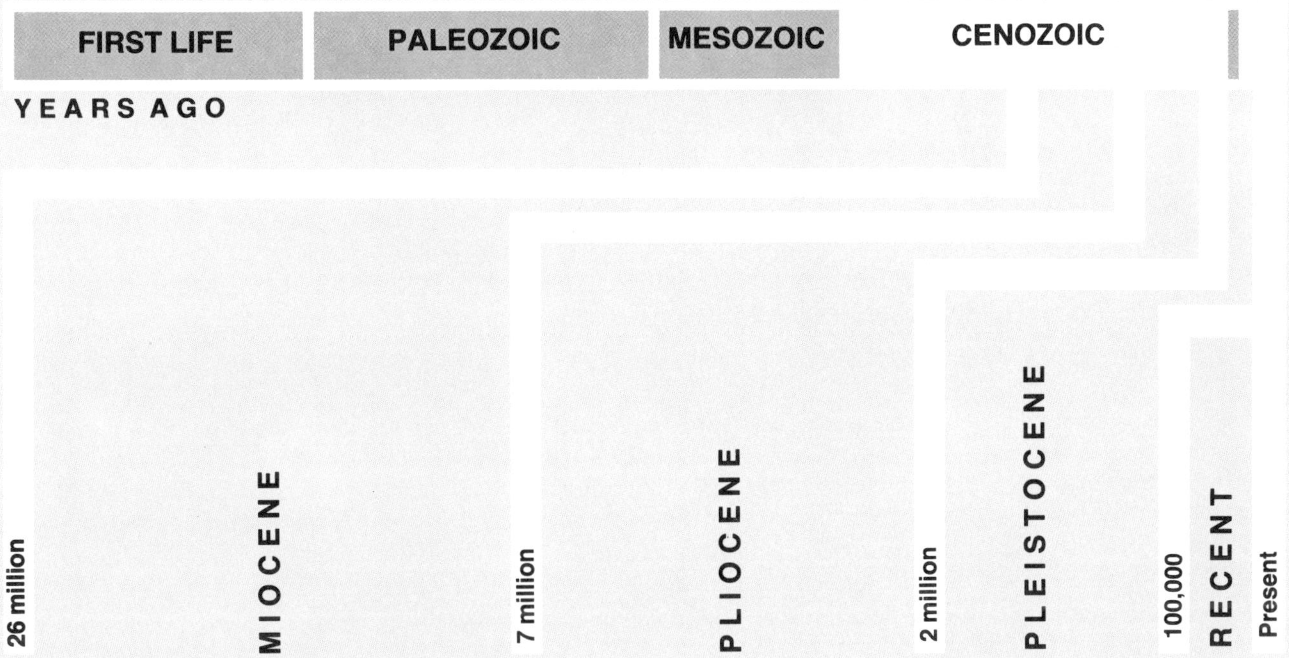

PART FOUR

THE HUMAN APE?

Arguably the Earth's most successful mammals, human beings evolved from ape-like creatures that lived on our planet over 20 million years ago. Since then they have come to dominate the Earth in a way that overshadows even the dinosaurs. They were the first creatures to discover fire, to make tools to help them in their search for food and shelter, and to wear clothes to keep them warm. They were the Earth's first artists, too, and yet their history is one of the shortest of any of the world's creatures. This then is the story of human beginnings, our story . . .

OUR DISTANT PAST

Humans belong to the ape group (called *Hominoidea*). We can begin the search for our evolutionary ancestors by looking for fossils of the first apes.

Fossils of various ape-like creatures have been found from the Miocene period, which began 26 million years ago. One of these was *Ramapithecus*, first found in India. Similar animals have also been found in other parts of Asia. They lived from about 14 million to about eight million years ago.

These early apes, often called 'ramapithecines', had certain similarities to humans. Whether they were our distant ancestors, we will probably never know. But they do give us an idea of how our ancestors might have evolved on the way to becoming human.

Ramapithecus lived at a time when the Earth's climate was becoming drier. The rain-loving forests that covered many tropical parts of the world were getting smaller, while grassland 'savannahs', dotted with trees, were spreading. So the ramapithecines had to change with the times in order to survive.

Ramapithecines, like other apes, were designed mainly for climbing in trees. But as trees became less common they would have had to spend more time on the ground. Many scientists think that the change from tree-living to ground-dwelling set the ramapithecines (or creatures like them) on the evolutionary path which led to the first humans.

A little can say a lot

Most of the fossils of *Ramapithecus* that have been found so far are only tiny fragments. Just one or two teeth, possibly with the piece of jaw bone in which they were fixed. One of the most 'complete' finds is most of a lower jaw. Hardly any other parts of the skeleton have been discovered.

But how can we tell what the ramapithecines looked like, and how they lived, from these few bits and pieces? By comparing these fossils with the same parts of other, better-known creatures, a little can say a lot.

The number and shape of the teeth show that *Ramapithecus* was definitely a primate. That means it belonged to the group that includes monkeys, apes and humans. But were they more closely related to apes or to us? The shape of the jaw suggests that the ramapithecines were on our side of the family tree, as you can see on the far right.

The way the teeth wear down also tells more than you might think. Imagine yourself chewing a tough bit of food. Your jaw moves up and down – and also from side to side. So your teeth wear down in an even, flat way. Modern apes don't move their jaws from side to side, only up and down – partly because their long canine teeth would get in the way.

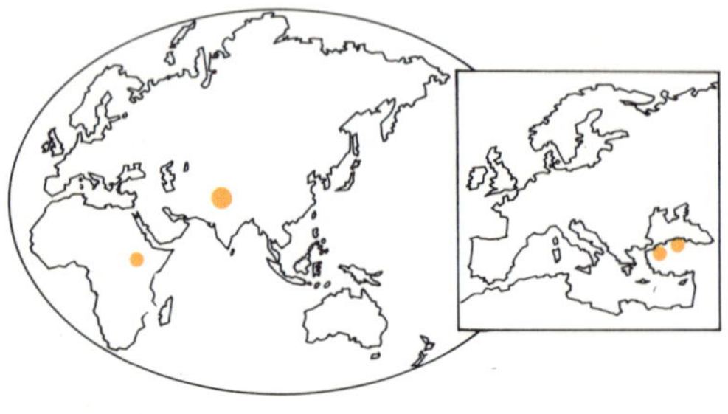

■ = Places where *Ramapithecus* remains have been found.

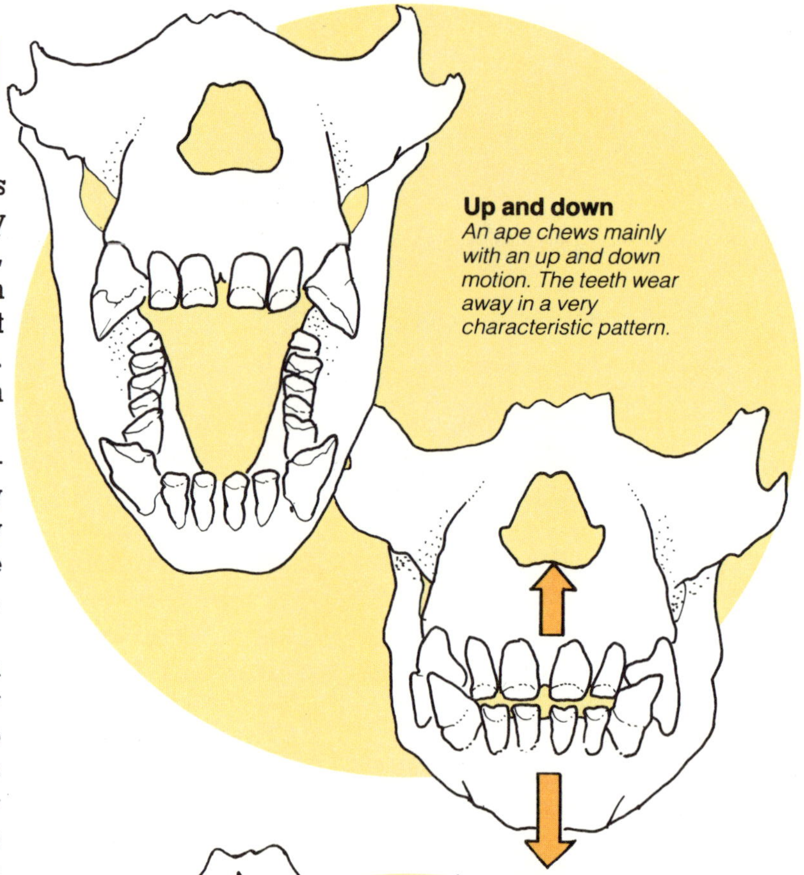

Up and down
An ape chews mainly with an up and down motion. The teeth wear away in a very characteristic pattern.

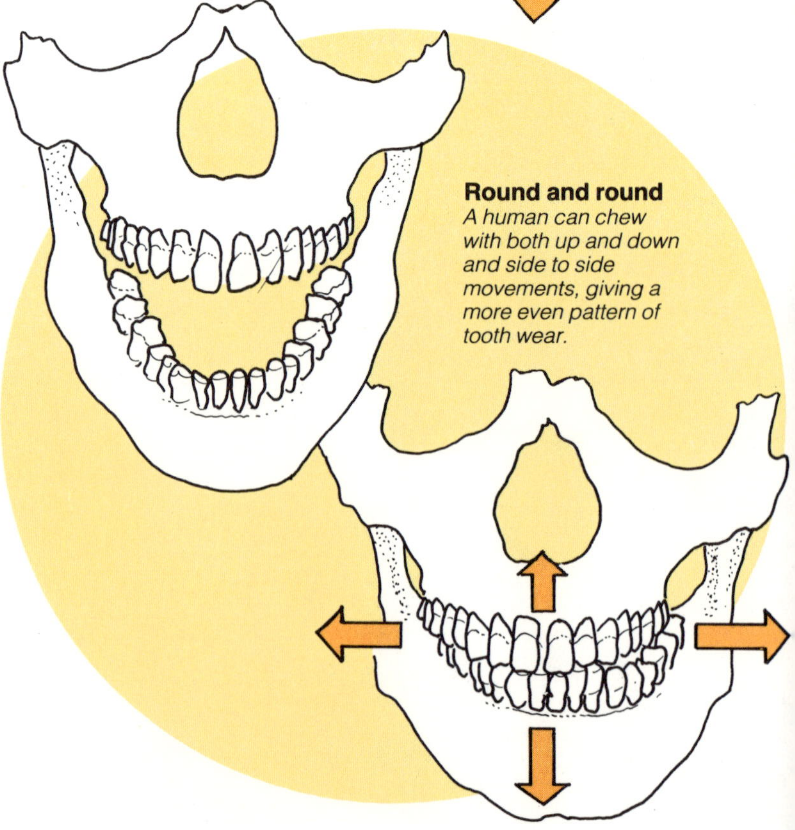

Round and round
A human can chew with both up and down and side to side movements, giving a more even pattern of tooth wear.

Their teeth wear down very unevenly, in grooves and pits. *Ramapithecus* teeth show a wear pattern that is more similar to our own that to a modern ape's.

Of course these clues only tell us that Ramapithecus was an ape-like creature from about 10 million years ago with jaws that looked and worked like ours. But it's a far cry from knowing that this prehistoric creature was our ancestor. The problem is that the fossil evidence is so small and broken-up that scientists can interpret it in several ways. When a new tooth or bit of jaw turns up, more often than not it doesn't clarify matters, but just gives room for new arguments.

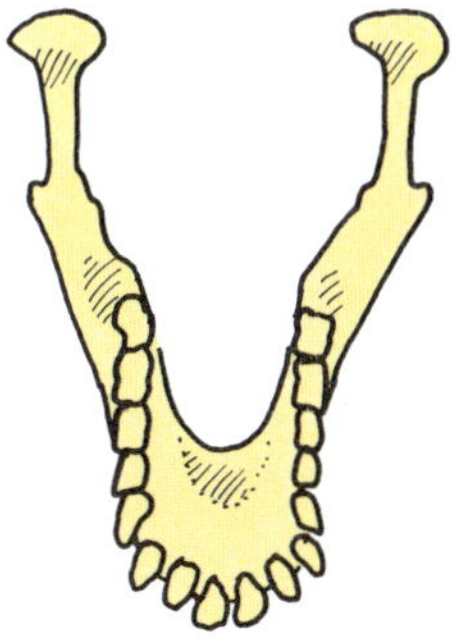

Modern ape's jaw
A modern ape such as a chimp has a large jaw that sticks out from the face. The sides of the jaw are parallel. The teeth, especially the canine teeth ('fangs'), are big in proportion to the jaw bone.

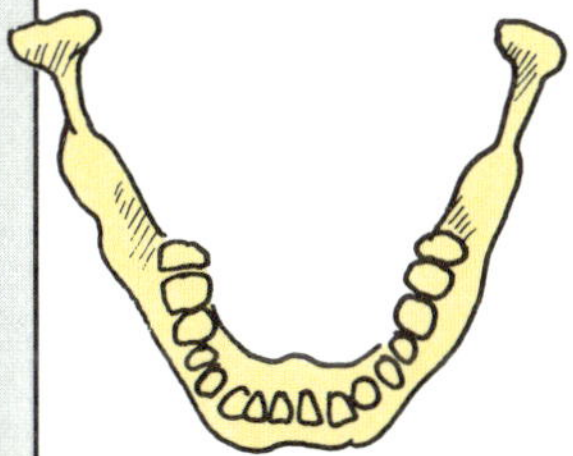

Human jaw
The jaw of a human is small and does not stick out much from the face. The sides of the jaw are not parallel – they form a curved shape. The teeth are quite small, and the canines aren't much bigger than the other teeth.

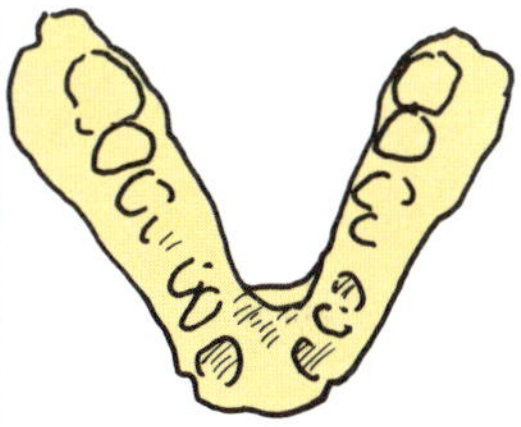

***Ramapithecus* jaw**
The ramapithecine jaw shows more similarities to a human than to a modern ape. It is not very large and its shape is more a curve, than the straight-sided U of an ape's jaw. The teeth are quite small too – the canines are only a little larger than the other teeth.

Before the chimp....

Proconsul is the name of a fossil ape from the Miocene period, about 20 million years ago. Its remains come from East Africa. This creature had many similarities to today's chimps. It was named after a very famous chimp called Consul who lived at London Zoo ('pro-' means 'before'). Like so many other fossil apes, its exact place in evolutionary history is uncertain. We are by no means sure that it was the ancestor of present-day chimps.

All apes together

We can look into the past, simply by looking around us today and finding animals that are similar to each other. Then we can try to work out which of their features have evolved recently, and which ones have been around for a long time – presumably inherited from a common ancestor.

There are five types of apes living today. One type is reading this – the human. The other four might qualify as being close relatives of ours. However the smallest apes, the gibbons of South-East Asia, are more monkey-like and are not generally thought to be very closely related to us. That leaves three others: orang-utans, chimps and gorillas.

Look at the pictures of these apes. You can immediately see obvious differences. Humans seem to have hardly any hair, while the others are quite furry. In fact this is not quite true. We actually have more hairs on our bodies than any of the other apes – but our hairs are much smaller and finer! So the nickname of the 'naked ape' for humans is not really correct.

There are plenty of other, more important, differences. We are upright, walking apes. The others are basically adapted for tree-climbing. Their arms are longer than their legs and they can swing through the trees with ease. They can grip with both their hands and their feet. When they move about on the ground it is usually on all fours, using their feet and the knuckles of

Today's apes
At first glance man looks very different from the other apes. But scientific study of bones, tissues and body chemistry shows that humans are very similar to chimps and gorillas.

their hands. The shape of the hip bone reflects this way of getting about, as does the position of the head on the backbone. Most of these differences can be traced back to the time when pre-humans came down out of the trees.

It is important to remember that, just as the human species has evolved over the past few million years, so have the other apes. The popular idea of humans evolving from chimpanzees, or other apes or monkeys that are alive today, isn't true. They have changed from the common ancestor, just as we have.

Which of the apes alive today is our closest relative? The evidence can be interpreted in different ways. Overall, if you include similarities in body chemistry (see right), the chimp may be our closest living relative.

Chemical clues

Many clues to evolution come from the shape and form of bones and other body parts. Recently scientists have come to realize that the 'shape' of chemical molecules inside the body can be just as revealing. The theory says the more similar a particular body chemical is in two animals, the more closely the animals are related.

For example, the chemical in blood called *haemoglobin*, carries oxygen from the lungs to all parts of the body. Haemoglobin has a complicated structure with over 500 'subunits', strung in lines like beads on lengths of string. The main form of haemoglobin in humans is identical to haemoglobin in chimpanzees. It is very unlikely that these haemoglobins evolved separately; it's much more probable that both humans and chimps inherited them from a common ancestor.

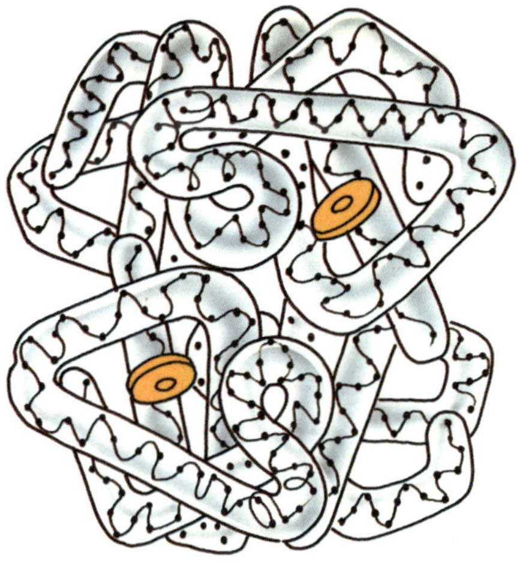

Haemoglobin molecule

The bigger brain

There are obvious differences in average brain size among the apes of today:

Gibbon ....about 90 mls (millilitres)
Chimp ....about 400 mls
Orang-utan ...about 450 mls
Gorilla ....about 500 mls
Human ....about 1300 mls

Even allowing for differences in body size, humans have by far the biggest brains in proportion to their bodies. Larger brains seem to be linked with greater intelligence. You can read about this on page 125.

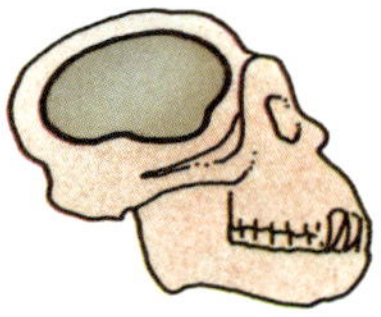

Gibbon

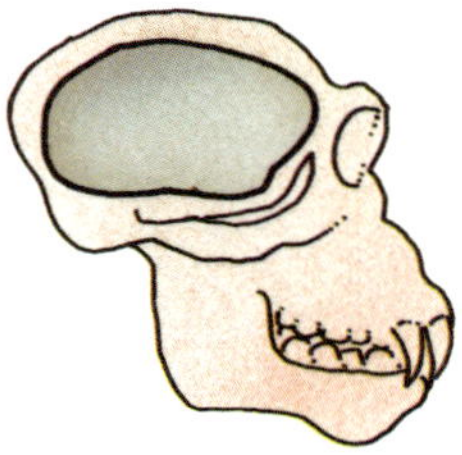

Chimpanzee

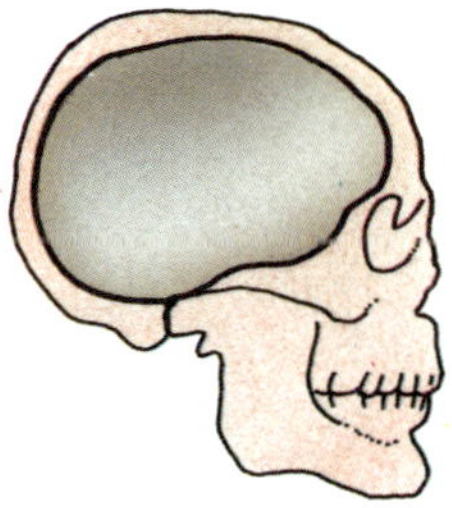

Human

A STEP CLOSER

By about four million years ago a new type of animal had evolved which had many human characteristics, although we would not call it human. This was *Australopithecus*, the 'southern ape'. Fossils of this creature have been found only in Africa.

Australopithecus had a fairly short muzzle (nose and mouth) compared to other apes, and its teeth had some human features. But it was only about the size of a chimpanzee, with a small brain – less than half the size of a human brain.

Some of the fossils are of the hip and leg bones. Their shapes show that *Australopithecus* could have walked comfortably on its legs alone. Apes walk awkwardly on their legs, and only for short distances. They prefer to shamble on all fours instead.

Any doubts about whether *Australopithecus* really could walk were swept away when a trail of fossil footprints was found at Laetoli, in Tanzania. These prints were left in mud about 3.7 million years ago by two *Australopithecus* individuals, as you can read on page 117.

Australopithecines were clearly neither humans nor apes, in the usual sense of the words. Some people call them 'ape-men' but this is not very scientific. So these creatures, and others similar enough to humans to be thought of as closely related to us, are included in the human family *Hominidae*. They are known as 'hominids'.

Ancestors of us all?

In 1924, in South Africa, Dr Raymond Dart found the first skull of *Australopithecus*. He soon realized its importance as one of the 'missing links' in the evolution of human beings. However, many of his fellow scientists were not convinced. They thought that the little skull, found in a quarry near Taungs, was of a type of chimpanzee. Other scientists unkindly called it 'Dart's baby'.

Today there is hardly any doubt that 'Dart's baby' was indeed a 'missing link'. Many fossils of *Australopithecus* and other prehumans and early humans have been dug up in East and South Africa.

One of the most famous and most complete specimens is also one of the oldest. This is 'Lucy', who lived about 3 million years ago in what is now Ethiopia. Her remains were discovered in 1974 by Dr Donald Johanson. What made them so exciting was that, besides the usual bits of teeth and skulls, there were also hip and limb bones. These showed Johanson that Lucy walked upright, or very nearly so.

Lucy shows a mixture of ape and human features. In particular, though, the hip bone is much more human than ape-like. So is the top of the femur (thigh bone). And the skull was sup-

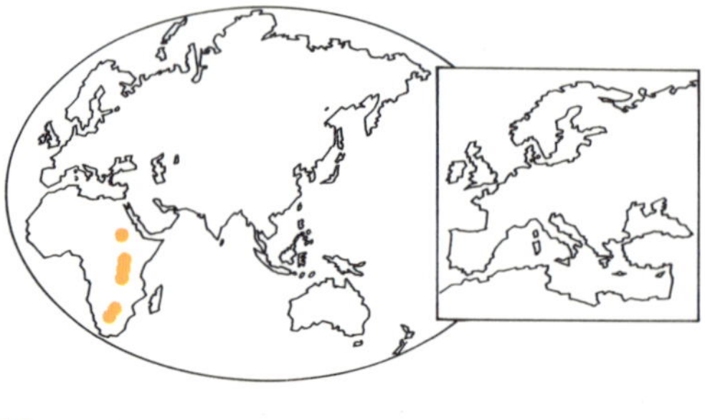

■ = Places where australopithecine fossils have been found.

A famous lady
'Lucy' is the most complete australopithecine yet discovered. In lif she was about 1.1 metres high, as tall a 7 year-old child of today, and weighed about 30 kilograms. The story is that she her nickname from th Beatles' song 'Lucy i the Sky with Diamonc which was playing ir the fossil-hunters' camp when her remains were found.

ported by the backbone from below, rather than at the back. There is little doubt Lucy could support all her weight on her legs and walk upright fairly easily.

Upright walking was, literally, a great stride forwards in evolution. The hands, freed from the need to help with movement by holding on to branches, could begin to explore, use and change objects. This ability may well have led to the evolution of a large brain and more intelligent behaviour, as you can read on page 125.

Some parts of Lucy were still rather ape-like. The head had a low forehead, large ridges over the eyebrows and a sticking-out jaw. Other parts were more human – the teeth were small and the jaw had a curved shape, not the straight-sided U of an ape.

As more australopithecine fossils are uncovered we can see that these hominids varied considerably. Different individuals seem to have a slightly different mix of features. We are almost certainly looking at more than one species. How many? You can find out on the next page.

Out for a stroll
The famous fossil footprints at Laetoli, mentioned on page 115, certainly show 'bipedal' locomotion' – walking on two legs. It cannot be proved that a creature like Lucy made them, but this seems extremely likely. Some scientists say the prints show signs of the toes curling. If so, this is an ape-like feature. Perhaps upright walking for an australopithecine was not quite as easy as it is for a modern human.

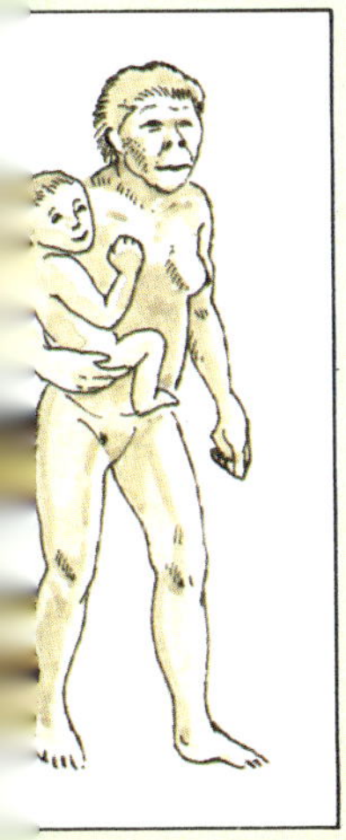

Human

Lucy

Gorilla

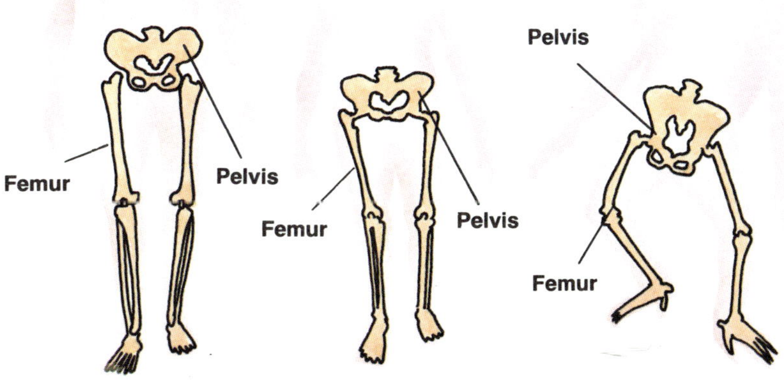

It's all in the hip!
Compare the tops of the thigh bones (called femurs) of a human, a gorilla and an australopithecine such as Lucy. In a human, the line of support goes straight up through the hip bone (pelvis) into the backbone. In a gorilla the femur is bent at an angle, since the ape tends to walk on all fours. Australopithecus had a femur much more like a human, which suggests upright walking.

How many australopithecines?

The basic groups of living things are called species. The first thing to do with almost any plant or animal is find out which species it belongs to. With fossils, though, it is not always easy to tell how many different species you are dealing with.

The modern definition of a species is a group of animals (or plants) that can breed together, to produce offspring that can also breed. Of course, fossils don't breed!

All animals in a species usually look very similar. Tigers are big and have stripes. Leopards – a different species – are smaller and have spots. But fossils have neither spots nor stripes. We don't get many clues from fossil bones and teeth about general appearance. Faced with only a few bones which could be of a tiger or a leopard, telling which animal it is becomes much more difficult. Is it a large, heavily-built leopard or a small tiger?

In many fossil collections, then, it is difficult to decide how many species there are. When looking at human evolution, it is even more awkward. Apart from a few specimens like Lucy, the only fossils are small scraps of skulls, jaws and teeth. It's no wonder that scientists differ in their opinions as to how many species of *Australopithecus* wandered across Africa in the last few million years.

Some fossil experts say there were two species of *Australopithecus*. Others say there were three. Some insist there were four, like we show here. Perhaps it is best, going on present evidence, to think of two main kinds of australopithecine – not necessarily two species. One type would be the *gracile* australo-

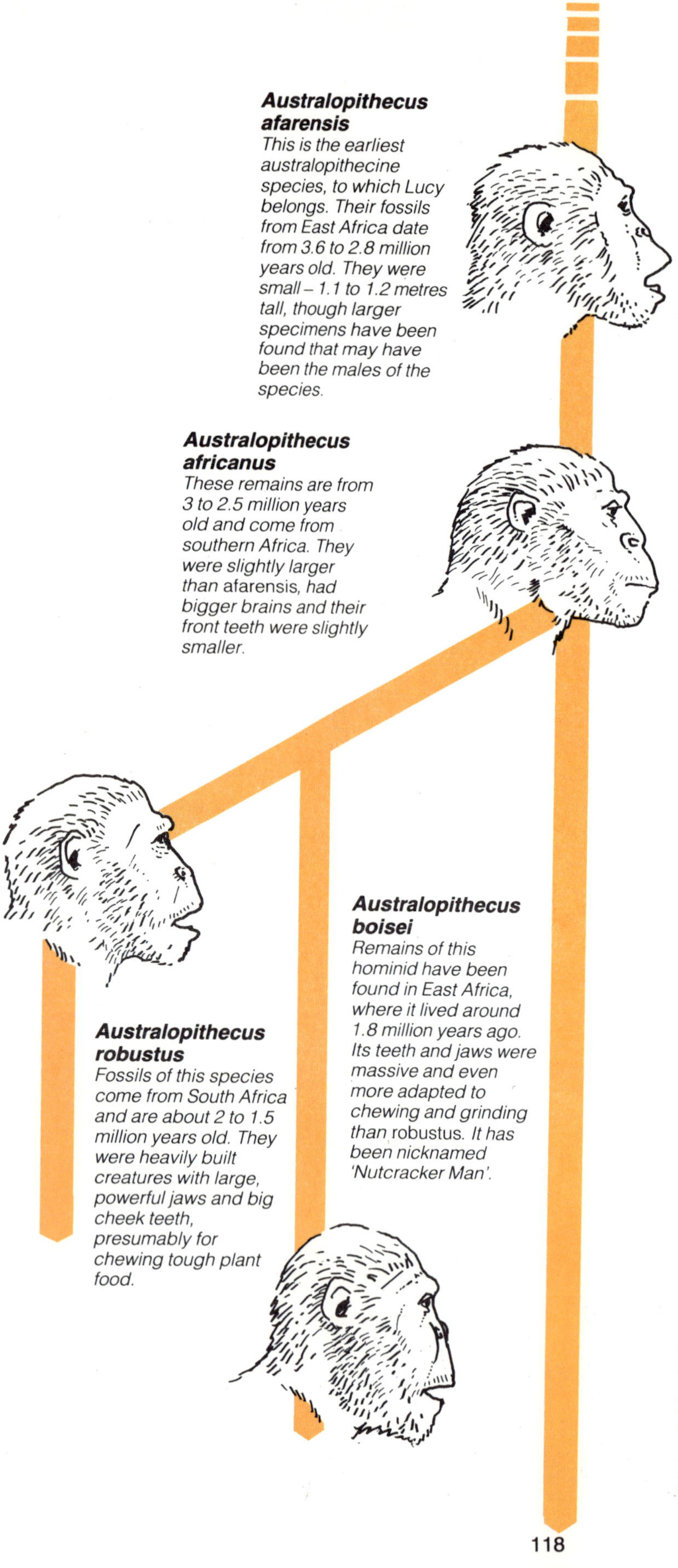

Australopithecus afarensis
This is the earliest australopithecine species, to which Lucy belongs. Their fossils from East Africa date from 3.6 to 2.8 million years old. They were small – 1.1 to 1.2 metres tall, though larger specimens have been found that may have been the males of the species.

Australopithecus africanus
These remains are from 3 to 2.5 million years old and come from southern Africa. They were slightly larger than afarensis, had bigger brains and their front teeth were slightly smaller.

Australopithecus boisei
Remains of this hominid have been found in East Africa, where it lived around 1.8 million years ago. Its teeth and jaws were massive and even more adapted to chewing and grinding than robustus. It has been nicknamed 'Nutcracker Man'.

Australopithecus robustus
Fossils of this species come from South Africa and are about 2 to 1.5 million years old. They were heavily built creatures with large, powerful jaws and big cheek teeth, presumably for chewing tough plant food.

Jaws for jobs

At one time, about 2 million years ago, *gracile* and *robust* australopithecines lived side by side in East Africa. The *robust* type had large jaws and strong, flat cheek teeth for chewing plant food. The *gracile* jaw was slimmer and lighter, and the teeth suggest a more mixed diet of plant and animal food.

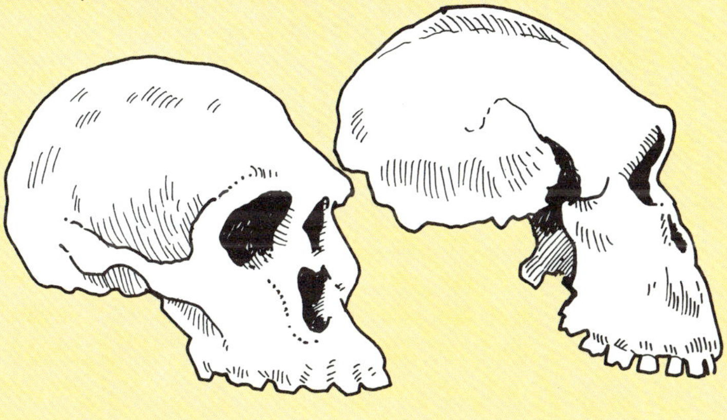

Skull of *gracile* australopithecine **Skull of *robust* australopithecine**

pithecine, lightly built and with a small jaw and teeth. *Afarensis* and *africanus* were in this group.

The other type would be the *robust* australopithecines, including *robustus* and *boisei*. As the name suggests they were larger, of heavier build and bigger-jawed. Both types showed a fair amount of variation between individuals, just as humans do today. They also lived alongside each other at some stage. The *robust* type specialized in plant-eating while the *gracile* type had a more general, mixed diet.

What happened to them? It seems that the *robust* australopithecines were too specialized to be our ancestors, and they probably died out. Perhaps their *gracile* relatives gradually won the battles for food or territories as they continued to evolve, as we can see in the next chapter.

Rooting for food
Nearly two million years ago the robust australopithecines wandered across Africa, looking for food such as roots and fruits.

THE FIRST HANDYMAN

Fossils show that about 1.8 million years ago, in East Africa, there lived a very human-like ape who could make and use tools. This is a human ability. Various animals, including chimps and some birds, use tools such as pebbles and twigs to help them obtain food. But only humans regularly take objects from their surroundings and change them, to make tools designed for a particular job.

The tool-maker from nearly two million years ago has been named *Homo habilis*. Some scientists believe he evolved from one species of *Australopithecus* (page 118). The tool-maker is thought to be related closely enough to us to be in the same genus, *Homo*, as modern man (*Homo sapiens*). The scientific name *Homo habilis* means 'Handy Man'.

'Handy Man' made fairly crude stone tools by hitting one flint against another, in such a way that flakes broke off, leaving a sharp edge for cutting or scraping. Tools like this are very sharp and effective.

At some places where 'Handy Man' tools are found, there are also remains of animal bones. Some bones have marks which were made by cutting – presumably the remains of food which was cut up by using the stone knives.

To go with his tool-making ability, 'Handy Man' seems to have had a larger brain than *Australopithecus*. But he was still only about 1.4 metres tall, like a 12 year-old child today.

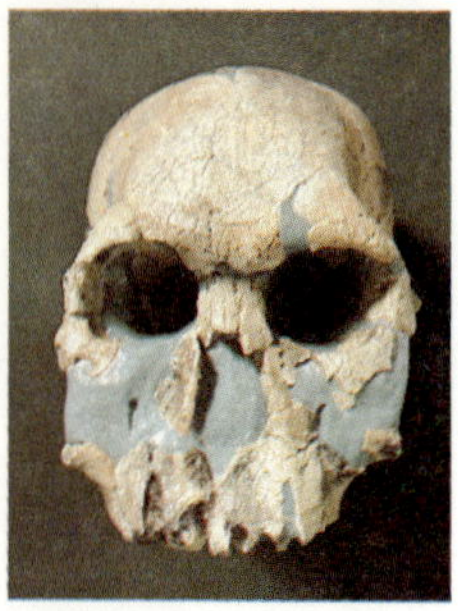

Getting ahead!
One of the most famous habiline fossils is this skull, known by its field code number '1470'. When it was discovered it helped to push back the beginnings of true humans by several hundred thousand years, to around 2 million years ago.

The first humans?

Following the discovery of the still ape-like australopithecines in Africa, and the much more human *Homo erectus* in Europe, East Asia and other places (page 127), there was still a gap or 'missing link' in the evolution of humans. The exciting finds of *Homo habilis* filled the gap.

The first specimens of 'Handy Man' (or the habilines, as fossil experts call them) were found in the early 1960s in Olduvai Gorge in Tanzania. More remains were discovered at Koobi Fora, in Kenya, and at Omo in Ethiopia. These fossils were mainly teeth, bits of skull and jaws, found in rocks from 2 to 1.5 million years old. They were somewhat similar to the australopithecine remains that were being found nearby. But it soon became clear that the habilines had bigger brains – 650 mls to 750 mls in volume.

One of the leading anthropologists (experts on human evolution and culture) is Richard Leakey, son of Louis and Mary (see right). He has discovered many remains of *Homo habilis* at Koobi Fora, as well as australopithecine fossils.

As usual, the picture is not as clear as we might hope. Some habiline fossils have big brains but not very human-looking jaws and teeth. Others have human-like jaws and teeth but small brains. As with *Australopithecus* it may be that there was more than one species of habiline. At the moment, we can't really say for sure.

What we can say is that just less than 2 million years ago in Africa, there were human-like apes with brains bigger than the australopithecines. They almost certainly made and used tools, as you can read on the next page. Gradually the gracile australopithecines faded out. After them, the more specialized, plant-eating, robust australopithecines also died out. *Homo habilis* may have helped to edge them to extinction. The scene was set for the humans to take over.

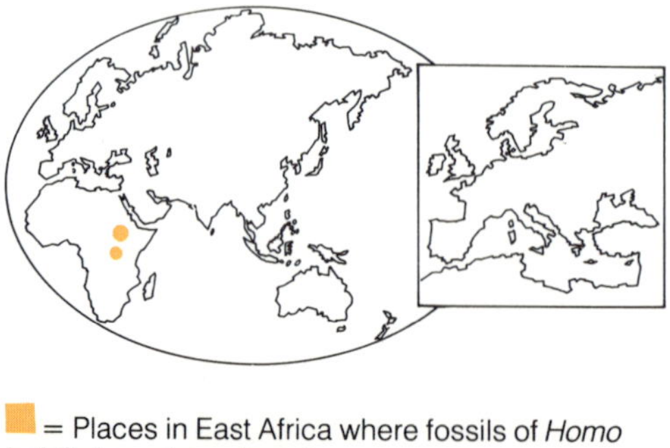

= Places in East Africa where fossils of *Homo habilis* have been found.

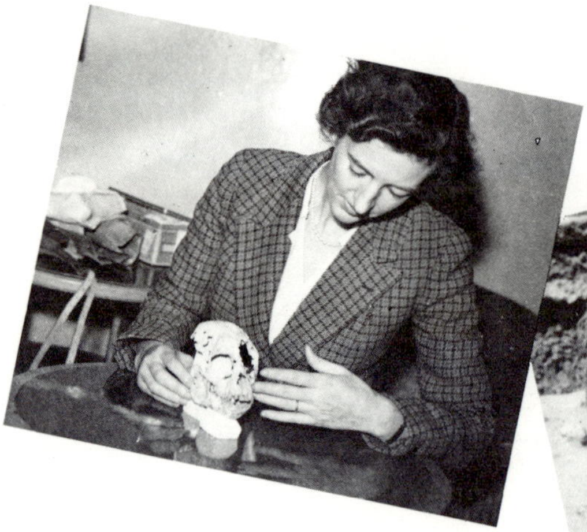

A fossil goldmine!

Near the wildlife-filled bowl of Ngorongoro Crater, in East Africa, is Olduvai Gorge. This steep valley is 40 kilometres long and in places 100 metres deep. About 2 million years ago the bottom of the gorge was the shore and bed of a lake. Since then it has been covered with layer upon layer of sedimentary rock, trapping and fossilizing whatever happened to be there. Then tremendous earth movements in the area (which is known as the Rift Valley) tore the ground apart to expose these ancient rocks.

Olduvai Gorge (right) is world famous for the discoveries of various hominid fossils, mainly by the palaeontologists Louis and Mary Leakey. Remains of many thousands of other animals, some new to science, have also been uncovered. 'Nutcracker Man' (page 118) was found here in 1959, and in 1960 the first specimen of *Homo habilis* was discovered.

Olduvai gorge

The Leakeys at work
The Leakey family has been among the foremost fossil experts and discoverers for many years. Mary (far left) examines a reconstructed skull; Louis (left) delicately picks at an embedded fossil; while their son Richard (below) studies a valuable site.

It's easy – with the right tools

The oldest tools in the world are the simple sharp-edged pebbles found at places like Olduvai Gorge. Some pebbles look like knives, possibly used for cutting through tough animal skin to get at the meat beneath. Others are more like scrapers, perhaps for scraping meat off animal bones. These tools were probably used like the Boy Scout's knife of today – for doing whatever is needed at the time.

Prehistoric tools are given certain names depending on how complicated and skilful their makers were. These earliest tools are known as 'Oldowan' (from Olduvai Gorge).

At one time it was thought that *Australopithecus* made these Oldowan tools. Now we believe that *Homo habilis* (Handy Man) made them. It is doubtful whether the small-brained australopithecines were clever enough to select a suitable stone, plan how to shape it, and then carefully chip away flakes to create something that would come in useful for a specific job in the future. Memory, abstract thought and hand-and-eye coordination are all needed to make tools.

It is unlikely that we will ever catch Handy Man 'red-handed' – that is, find a fossil of *Homo habilis* with a stone tool actually in his hand. So we can never be sure the habilines really did make the tools. But the tools are found in rocks of a similar age to the habiline remains (up to 2 million years old) and in similar places. The conclusion that the experts have come to, is that the habilines were the first tool-makers.

Oldowan tools have also been found in Ethiopia in rocks that may be up to 2.5 million years old. This is half a million years before the first fossils of *Homo habilis* yet discovered. Did some of the australopithecines make tools then? It's more likely that the habilines were alive at this time, and we have yet to find their remains.

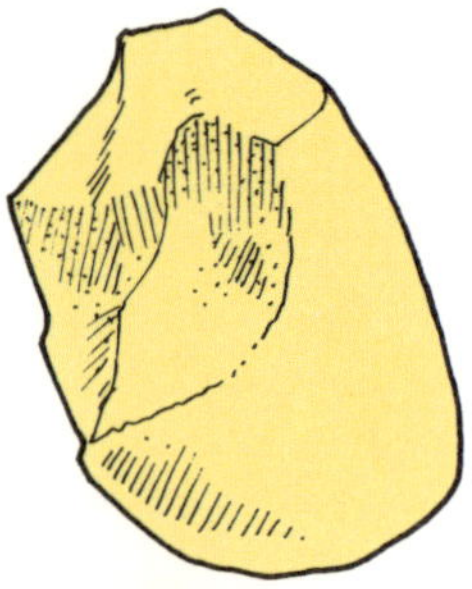

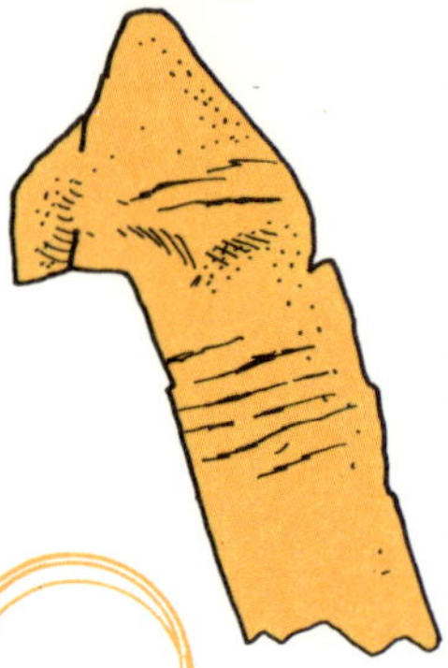

Stones *and* bones?
Scientists are fairly certain that the habilines used chipped pebbles as tools. Whether they used broken bones as clubs or gougers is more debatable.

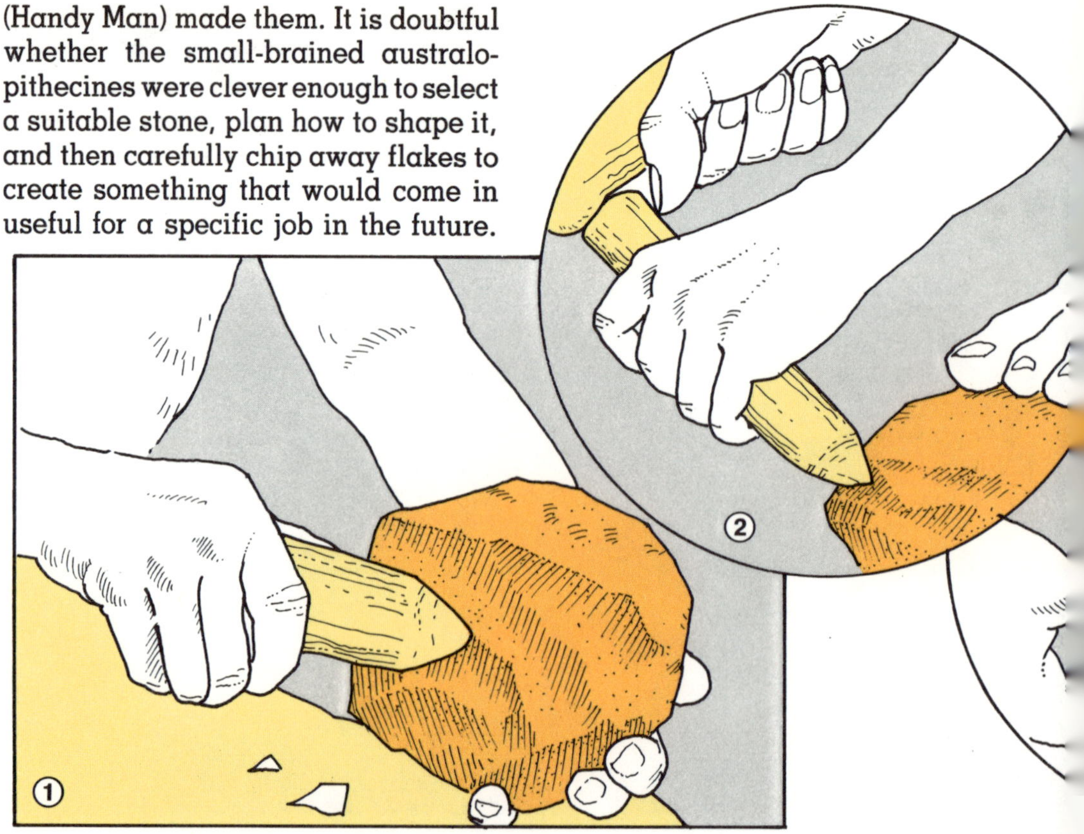

Are big brains best?

Soft parts of animals, such as the brain, quickly rot away and are not preserved. So how do we know the size of a creature's brain from fossils? The answer is that although the brain itself is not there, the space into which it fitted – the inside of the skull – may be. If a fossil skull is fairly complete it is possible to measure the inside volume of the *cranium* (brainbox). By making a small allowance for the fluid and membrane, we can calculate the volume of the brain itself.

But does a bigger brain mean higher intelligence? In living humans this is not necessarily so. Neither is it the case in other animals – or the big whales, with the biggest brains of all, would be far cleverer than us.

Even so, in human evolution the size of the brain and, more importantly, the size of the brain in proportion to the rest of the body, seems to be connected with intelligence.

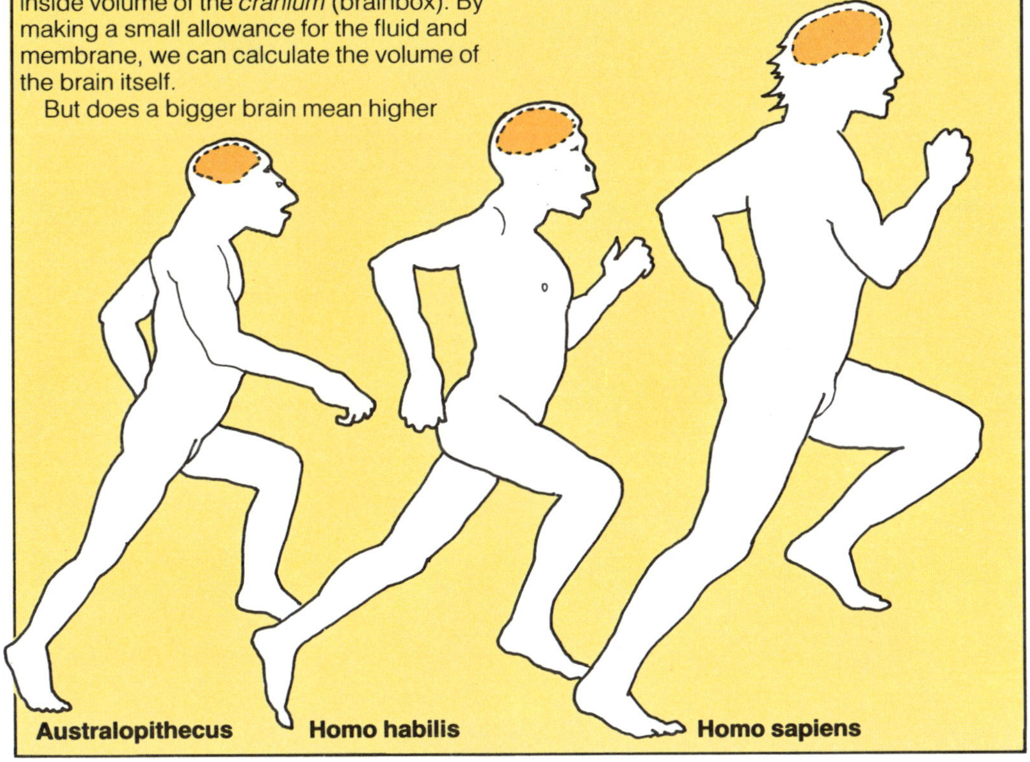

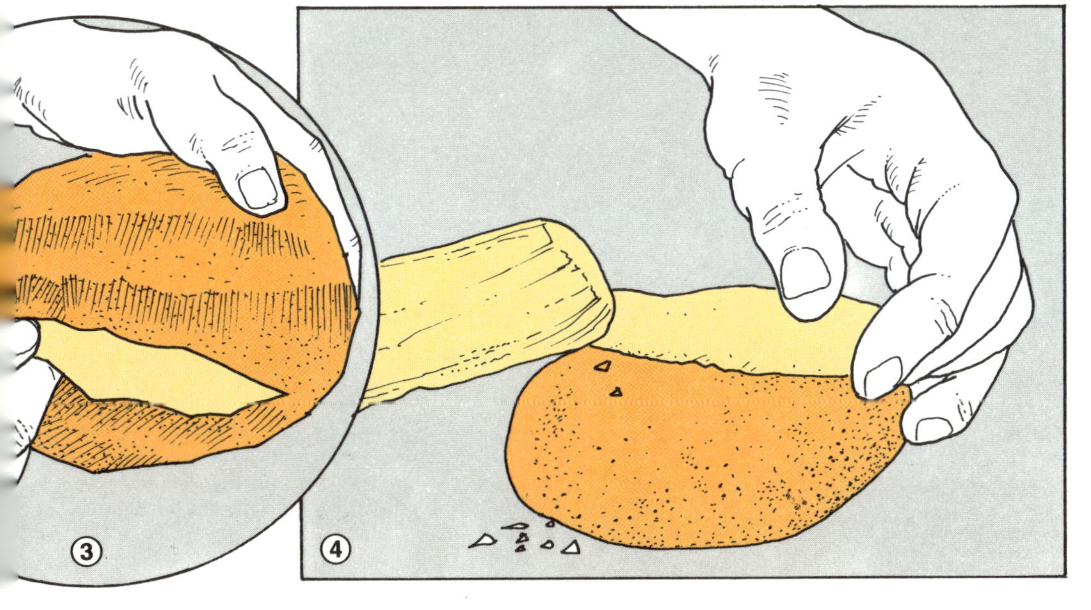

Working in stone

1 *Using a piece of bone or antler as a hammer allows finer shaping of a flint, removing only small pieces.*
2 *Hitting a bone chisel with a hammer gives very accurate splitting of the flint.*
3 *A razor-thin blade of flint is detached by a hammer blow.*
4 *One edge of the blade can be blunted by small taps with a bone hammer, so that it can be held safely in the hand.*

OUT OF AFRICA

The early hominids, *Australopithecus* and *Homo habilis*, lived in Africa. The first people we know of who moved out of this continent belong to a group named *Homo erectus* – meaning 'Upright Man'. These people were similar to ourselves in body size. But the main differences were in their skulls and teeth. These have been found to be not quite like those of modern humans, and their brains were only about two-thirds the size of ours.

The oldest *Homo erectus* fossils are from about 1.5 million years ago and were found in Africa, so these people probably evolved there. But by one million years ago they had spread to southern Asia, and later remains have been found in northern China and Europe.

One of the most famous fossils of *Homo erectus* is 'Peking Man' (page 131), found in a prehistoric cave near Peking in China. People like him not only made good stone tools, including beautifully-shaped hand-axes, but they also used fire. The cave near Peking contains the remains of charcoal, burnt bones, and layers of ash. This means that the *erectus* people could use and control fire – probably for cooking, and to help them keep warm in what was a fairly cool climate.

The cave remains tell us that the Peking people had stayed in one place for a time. These upright, tool-making, fire-using humans had begun to have 'homes'.

The first campfires

Northern China in winter can be a cold place. To the 'naked ape' *Homo erectus*, with his early glimmerings of human intelligence and resourcefulness, anything that made life a little easier would be worth investigating. A forest fire started by the lightning bolt of an autumn thunderstorm ... that felt warm ... what if the fire was fed with sticks and kept going in one place? Then the long winter nights might not be so cold.

A far-fetched story, perhaps. But the evidence that Peking Man used fire is strong. We don't know whether he could actually make fire whenever he wanted to, or whether he had just learned to keep a fire going after it had been started by some natural means. Yet the evidence of various finds at caves in Choukoutien and elsewhere gives strong clues to the use of fire. Ash, charcoal and burnt bones have been discovered – presumably the remains of a 'camp fire' and the meal cooked there.

Scorched stones have also been found at the 'camp sites'. Did these people make 'ovens' out of hot stones? Perhaps they dropped hot stones into water, to heat it for cooking. If so, they must have had some kind of water vessel – perhaps even a hole in the ground or a hollow in a rock.

And associated with many *erectus* finds are his characteristic tools. These are Acheulean hand-axes, which are named after a place in France where many have been found. The axes are usually chipped to a pointed pear shape. They first appear in the fossil record about 1.5 million years ago and continue in much the same form for a million years. Hand axes have been collected from many parts of the world, including some parts of Europe where fossils of *Homo erectus* himself have yet to be detected.

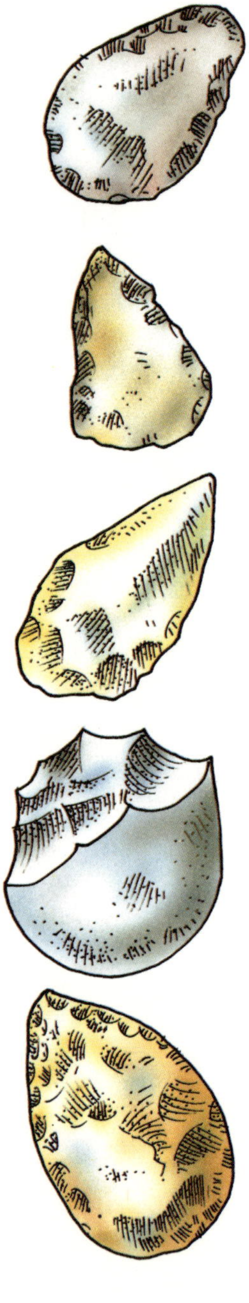

Acheulean tools
The well-shaped tools of the erectus people were a great improvement on the roughly-hewn pebbles of the habilines.

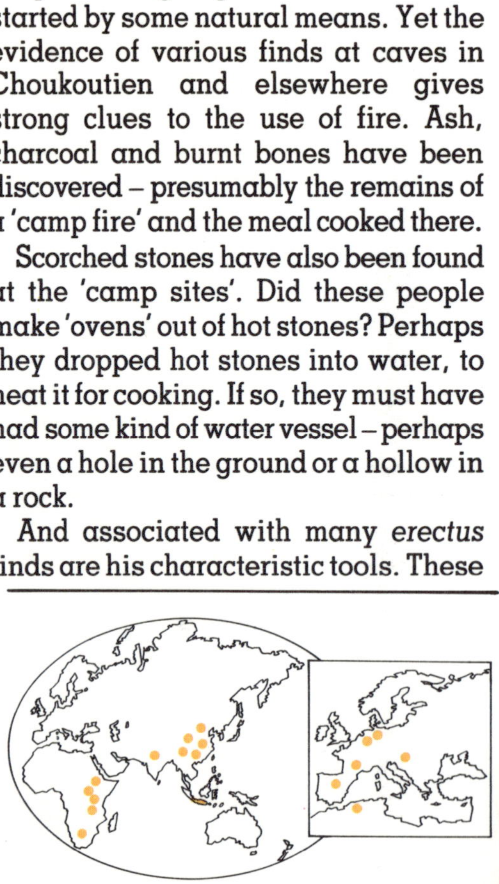

■ = Places where fossils or signs of *Homo erectus* have been found.

On present evidence, 'Upright Man' seems to have evolved in Africa. Then groups began to spread across the world. They arrived in Europe perhaps 800,000 years ago. These people were intelligent and adaptable enough to survive away from the warmth and plentiful food of the tropics. According to some scientists, *Homo erectus* had virtually died out about 300,000 years ago. Yet in one sense he still lives – since he evolved into us.

An all-purpose tool
Like the roughly-shaped pebbles of Homo habilis, *the 'hand-axe' of* Homo erectus *was probably a tool for many jobs – cutting, skinning, chipping, hacking and levering. The workmanship of some specimens is beautiful. The finished axe fits snugly in the hand and is well balanced. Not many of our tools will be around in a million years!*

Walking tall

The oldest and most complete fossils of *Homo erectus* were found at Lake Turkana in Kenya, in 1984. Looking particularly at the teeth and the development of the hip bone, the remains are probably of a 12 year-old boy. He was 1.6 metres high – as tall as a 12-year-old boy today.

In fact, apart from the bones being a bit thicker and rougher, they are very similar to ours. The only big difference is in the skull. The forehead is low and there are thick ridges at the eyebrows. This youngster's brain volume was between 900 and 1,000 mls – much bigger than *Homo habilis*, but smaller than modern man's. The body was almost that of modern man, but the brain still had some evolving to do.

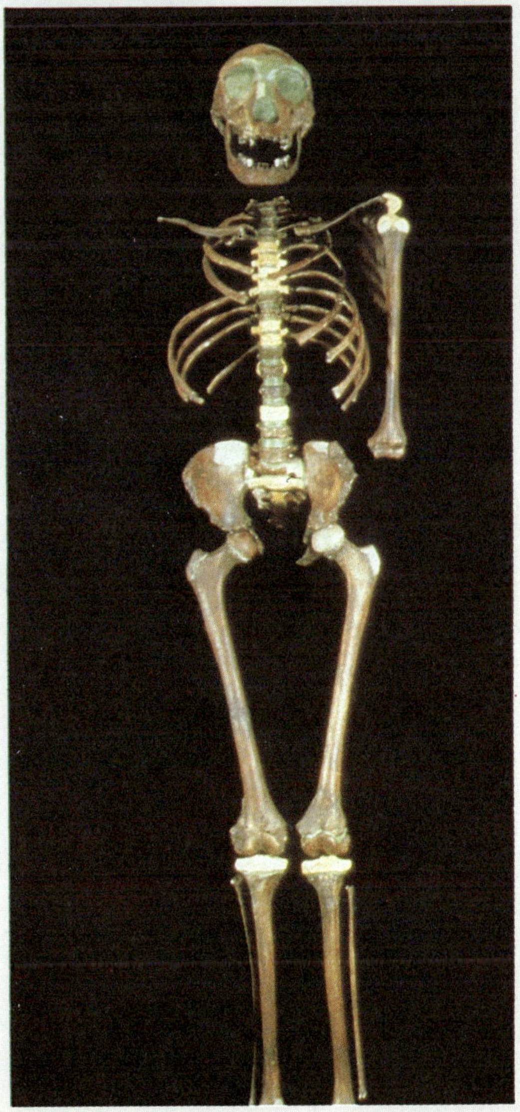

How many 'ape-men'?

Where did we come from? This question has always had a peculiar fascination for humans. Yet delving into the evolutionary clues has not produced a neat, cut-and-dried answer. Fossils of our ancestors are fragmentary, few and far between. Ideas and theories about how we evolved have changed many times in the past, and there is no reason to think we have the right answers now.

Science first started taking evolution seriously when the famous naturalist Charles Darwin wrote about his ideas in his book *On the Origin of Species*. At that time, in 1859, only one type of fossil man had been found – Neanderthal Man (page 138). Virtually all we know today about the various extinct hominids has been discovered in the past hundred years, and much of it only in the past thirty years.

In the early days of fossil-hunting for our ancestors, there was hardly any 'framework of knowledge' into which discoveries could be fitted. There were no similar finds that could be compared, so scientists were free to make their own interpretations. Also, some of the collectors were keen to make a name for themselves and be the discoverer of the fabled 'missing link'. As a result,

Piltdown's discoverer
Charles Dawson was a lawyer who searched for fossils in his spare time. He found the first scraps of fossils on Piltdown Common in 1908.

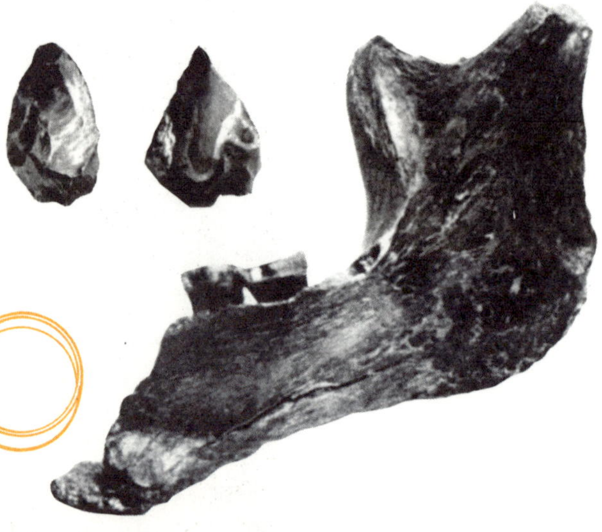

The hoax of Piltdown Man

The infamous 'fossils' of Piltdown Man were discovered in 1912 in a gravel pit in Sussex, England, by Charles Dawson – an amateur geologist. Over a period of time several fossil pieces were dug up from the gravel. They were brown with age and when put together they formed almost a complete human-like skull and ape-like lower jaw. Many scientists were waiting for such a find – a primitive man from hundreds of thousands of years ago with a large brain but ape-like jaws and teeth. So they hailed the discovery as the true 'missing link', and ignored others who wondered if the skull and jaw really belonged together.

In the 1940s the technique of fluorine dating was developed. Fossils absorb the chemical fluorine from the soil, and the longer they are new species and groups were named on the slenderest evidence.

Hunting for the past has also been affected by the world of the present – several valuable fossil collections were lost in the Second World War, and 'digs' have had to be stopped due to outbreaks of fighting.

New finds are being made all the time. Gradually, though, the picture is becoming simpler. As more remains are found and studied, the experts come to recognize similarities between specimens and we can see the general pattern of evolution more clearly. On the right is a timetable of some of the more important hominid finds in the past hundred or so years.

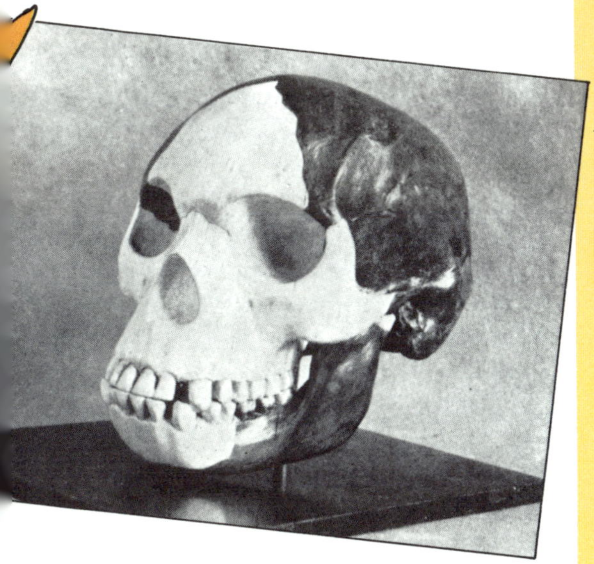

buried the more fluorine they contain. Piltdown Man was tested. The skull and jaw contained hardly any fluorine. Then the technician doing the test noticed that the brown colour was only on the surface of the bones. Underneath they were white and new.

Piltdown Man was exposed as a trick. The remains were actually only abut 500 years old. The skull was of a man, and the jaw was from an orang-utan, with the teeth filed down to make them look human. Both had been stained brown to make them look old and 'planted' in the gravel pit.

To this day no one knows who played this trick, which fooled the world's human evolution 'experts' for over thirty years.

Hominid names – then and now

Year	Find	Scientific name then	Scientific name now
1856	Neanderthal Man	*Homo neanderthalensis* 'Man of the Neander Valley'	*Homo sapiens neanderthalensis* 
1891	Java Man	*Pithecanthropus erectus* 'Upright Ape-Man'	*Homo erectus* 
1912	Piltdown Man	*Eoanthropus* 'Dawn Man'	(See below left)
1924	Taung child	*Australopithecus africanus* 'South African ape'	*Australopithecus africanus* 
1929	Peking Man	*Sinanthropus pekinensis* 'China Man of Peking'	*Homo erectus* 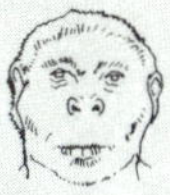
1938	Kromdraai Man	*Paranthropus robustus* 'Robust Near-Man'	*Australopithecus robustus* 
1959	Nutcracker Man	*Zinjanthropus*	*Australopithecus boisei* 
1960	Handy Man	*Homo habilis*	*Homo habilis* 
1974	Lucy	*Australopithecus afarensis*	*Australopithecus afarensis* 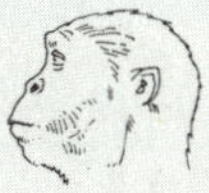

Our ancestral past–today!

Before we look at the beginnings of our own species, *Homo sapiens*, let's sum up what we know about our past. The evolutionary tree' shown here is one acepted by many scientists – on today's evidence.

Our distant past, possibly involving creatures like *Ramapithecus*, is very sketchy. After this the line of descent runs from *Australopithecus afarensis* through to *Homo sapiens*. As mentioned on page 118, some experts say there weren't four separate species of *Australopithecus* – perhaps two. Also by no means everyone believes that *Australopithecus* evolved into *Homo habilis*. Some say that we should expect to find a 'prehominid' further back in time that was the ancestor of both *Australopithecus* and *Homo habilis*. This would mean that *Australopithecus* wasn't on the line of evolution leading to modern man.

Most scientists believe that *Australopithecus robustus* and Neanderthal Man were evolutionary dead-ends. But the idea of *habilis* evolving into *erectus* evolving into *sapiens* has fairly general agreement.

From about 500,000 to 30,000 years ago the picture is confused. Some of the fossils show mixed features of *erectus* and Modern man. What was happening? There are two main ideas:

One says that once *Homo erectus* evolved, he spread across the world and then these different groups changed into *Homo sapiens*, perhaps at different speeds. So modern man arose several times in several places.

The second view is that *erectus* evolved into *sapiens* in one place – probably Africa. Then several 'waves' of *sapiens* people migrated to other countries and any *erectus* people already living there died out. Some *sapiens* reached Australia possibly 40,000 years ago. Others went via Eastern Asia into America, perhaps about 30,000 to 20,000 years ago. Still others entered Europe around 30,000 years ago. You can read about these people on the next pages.

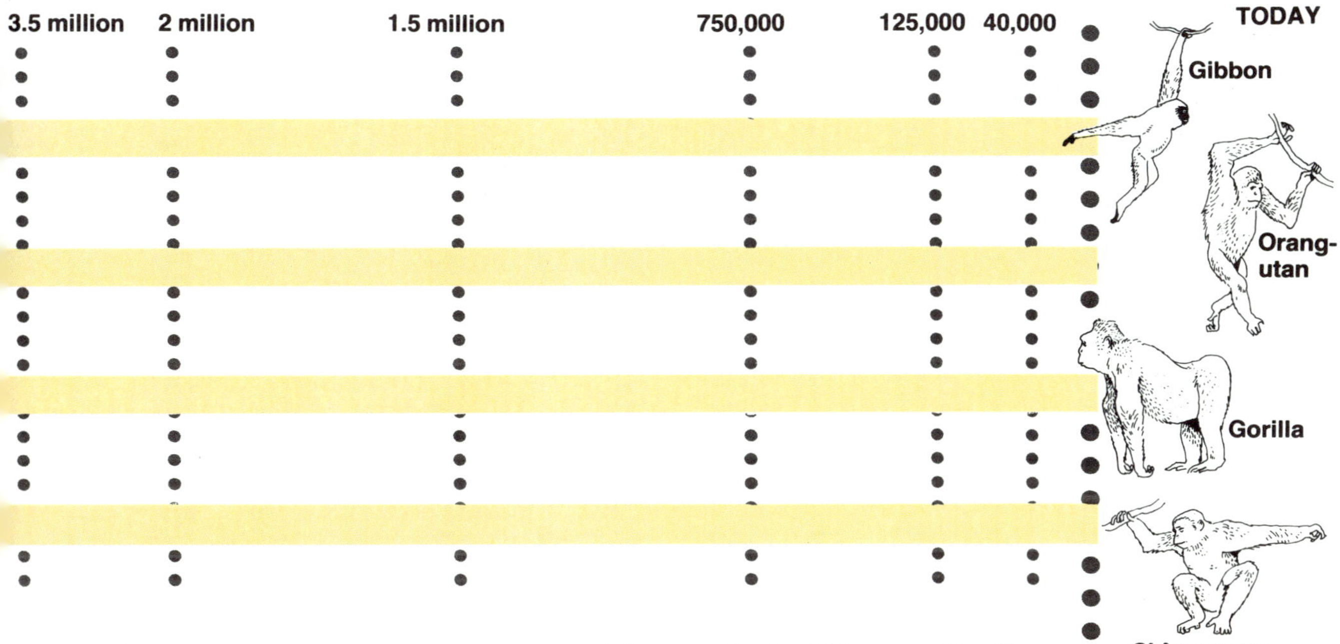

The big split

When trying to sort out our history, it can be helpful to look at the evolution of the other great apes. When did their evolutionary line split away from ours?

Fossil experts used to say that the chimp, gorilla and orang-utan went off on their own evolutionary path about 20 or even 30 million years ago. But the evidence from body chemicals (page 113), as well as a new look at old fossils, puts this split much nearer to today – at 10 to 7 million years ago. This idea of a recent split, say around 10 million years ago, is gradually becoming more widely accepted. If this is true, it means that evolution can work faster than we had thought.

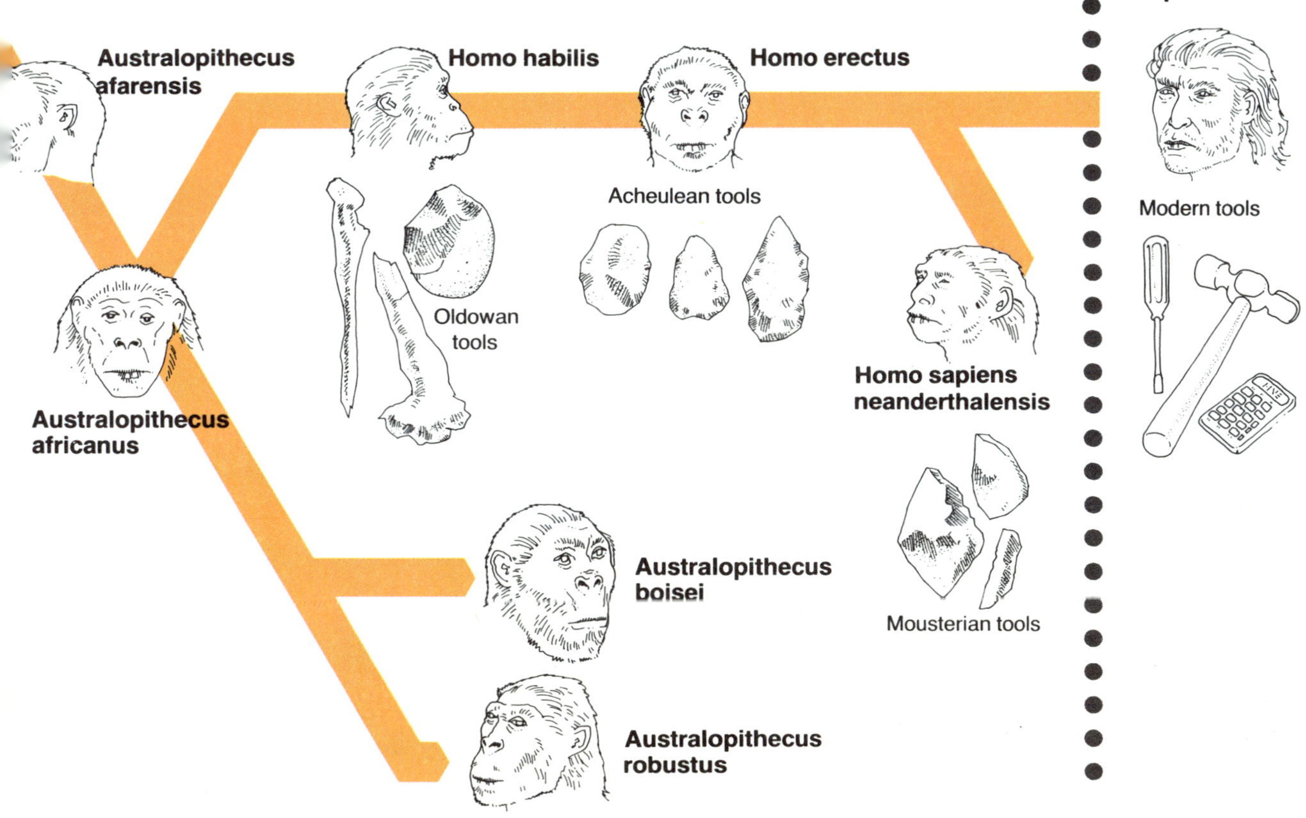

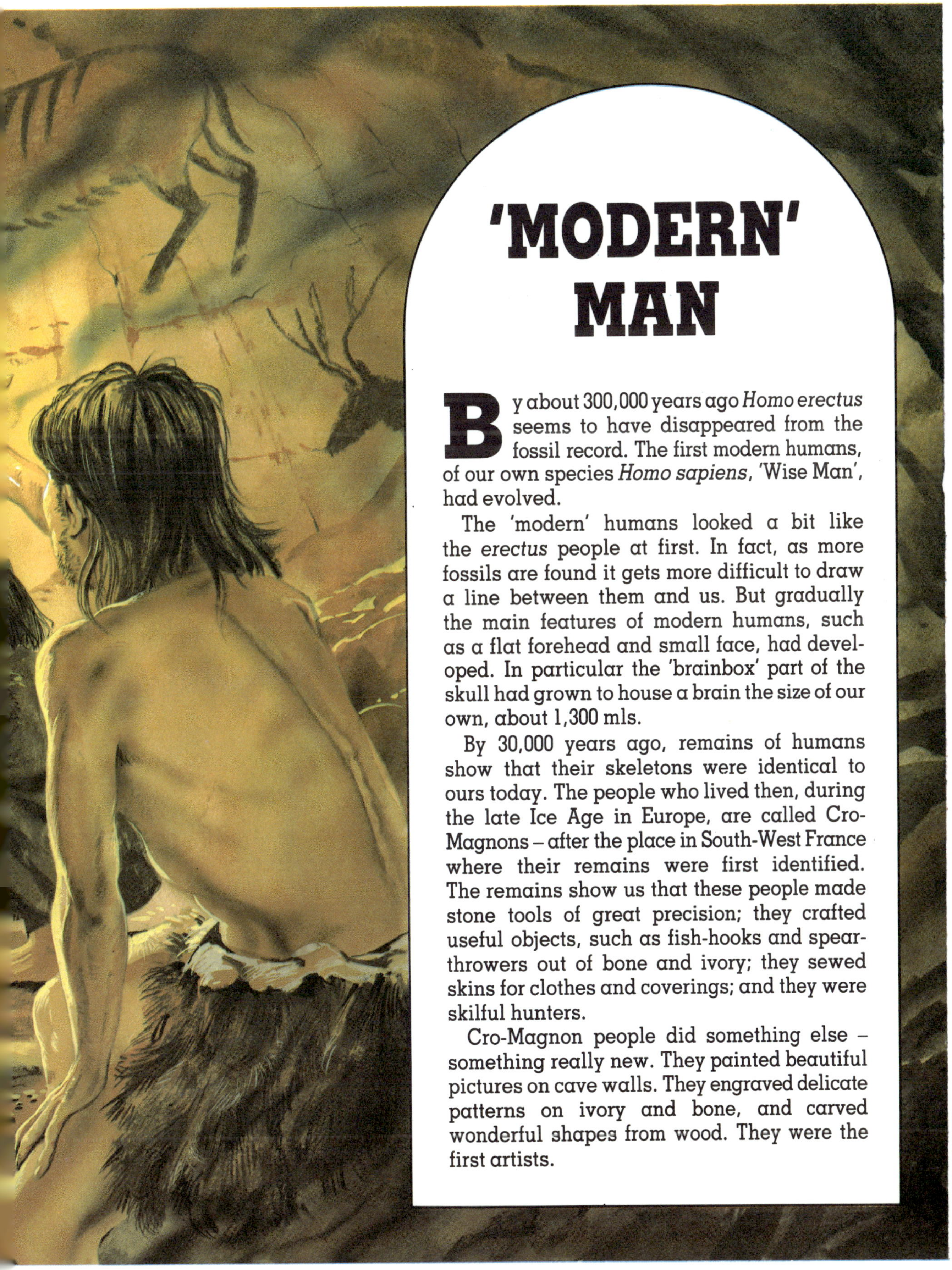

'MODERN' MAN

By about 300,000 years ago *Homo erectus* seems to have disappeared from the fossil record. The first modern humans, of our own species *Homo sapiens*, 'Wise Man', had evolved.

The 'modern' humans looked a bit like the *erectus* people at first. In fact, as more fossils are found it gets more difficult to draw a line between them and us. But gradually the main features of modern humans, such as a flat forehead and small face, had developed. In particular the 'brainbox' part of the skull had grown to house a brain the size of our own, about 1,300 mls.

By 30,000 years ago, remains of humans show that their skeletons were identical to ours today. The people who lived then, during the late Ice Age in Europe, are called Cro-Magnons – after the place in South-West France where their remains were first identified. The remains show us that these people made stone tools of great precision; they crafted useful objects, such as fish-hooks and spear-throwers out of bone and ivory; they sewed skins for clothes and coverings; and they were skilful hunters.

Cro-Magnon people did something else – something really new. They painted beautiful pictures on cave walls. They engraved delicate patterns on ivory and bone, and carved wonderful shapes from wood. They were the first artists.

The Cro-Magnon people

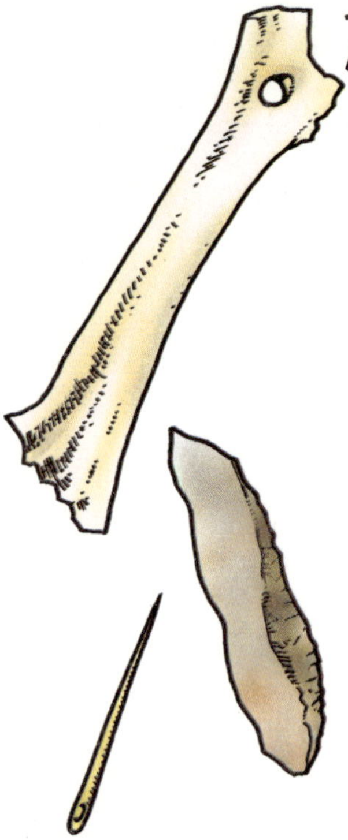

The first Cro-Magnon remains were uncovered in 1868, as workmen dug a railway cutting in the Dordogne region of France. Other remains were found in nearby places and also in Spain. As more discoveries were made around the world, many more finds of similar age came to light. They were between 35,000 and 10,000 years old. Our own sub-species of modern man, *Homo sapiens sapiens*, was truly on the map.

These early modern men seem to have lived in groups perhaps 50 or more strong. With their remains are those of deer, horses and bison – no doubt the results of hunting. While Cro-Magnons lived in Europe the great Ice Age came and went, and there is evidence they hunted the huge woolly mammoths that also lived on the Earth then.

Do it yourself
This early 'tool kit' would allow Cro-Magnon man to carry out a range of jobs around the home. The 'baton' (bone with hole) at the top may not have been a tool, but a symbol of authority.

Cro-Magnons left examples of their artistry on cave walls in Southern France and Spain. 'Stone-age' art is also found around the Sahara in North Africa. A great deal of effort went into these paintings. The colours were made by crushing rocks to get pigments. The yellows and reds came from iron oxides and black from manganese oxides. The coloured powders were mixed with animal fats to make paint. Designing the pictures and drawing them in the darkness of a cave must have taken a lot of trouble.

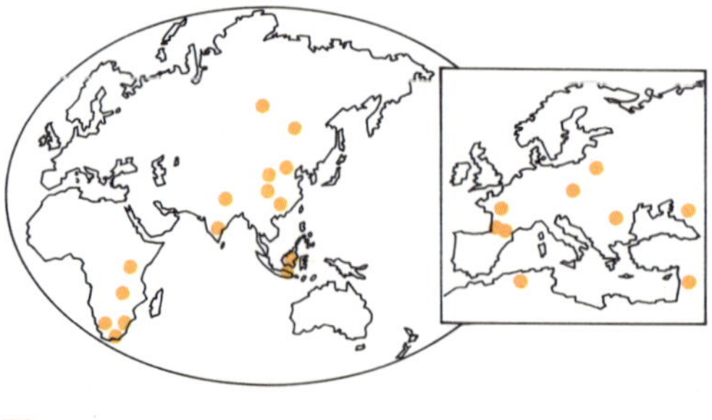

■ = Places where fossils or signs of Cro-Magnon man have been found.

So why did the Cro-Magnons make their paintings? The animals in them are mostly the ones they hunted, and some appear to have been speared. The pictures probably had some sort of magical or ritual meaning. Drawing a bison with a spear stuck in it could have given you good luck in a coming hunt. The Cro-Magnon people used symbols to express their thoughts. As well as painting, they engraved their hunting weapons with patterns and pictures.

Certain remains appear to be of Cro-Magnon cemeteries. The individuals were placed on their sides with their knees tucked under their chin, and weapons or tools were buried with them. In fact the first skeletons to be discovered had almost certainly been deliberately buried.

Prehistoric paintings
Cro-Magnon cave art usually shows animals that were hunted for food. The work on the left is from Altamira in Spain; the picture above comes from Lascaux in France.

The language of humans

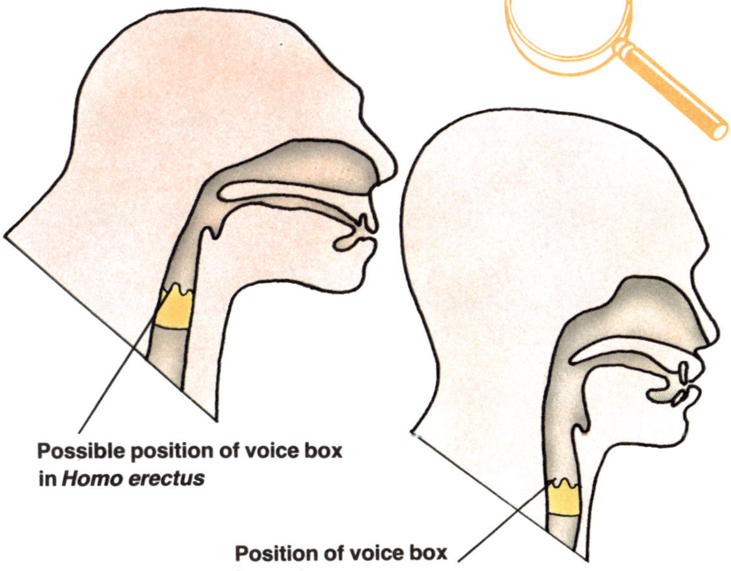

How long have humans been using language? Simple sounds like grunts and screeches were probably used by *Homo habilis* and maybe even *Australopithecus*. But complex languages with hundreds of different words may be fairly recent.

In babies today, the voice box or *larynx* is in a high position up near the skull. Only after a year or so does it sink lower, more into the neck. Then the baby begins to talk. The position of the voice box may be important in speaking clearly. In today's apes the voice box is in a similar high position and never sinks down – and apes can't talk like us.

Fossil evidence shows that in *Homo erectus*, the voice box was also in a high position. So he might only have been able to speak in a clumsy, simple way. Once the voice box had evolved into a more suitable position in the neck, in *Homo sapiens*, better speech was possible.

The cavemen who missed out?

Think of the popular cartoon image of a caveman: short, stooping, stocky and stupid. This image comes from the interpretations of the fossils of Neanderthal Man, but as we shall see it isn't true. The Neanderthals were our very close cousins, belonging to our species *Homo sapiens* but as a different sub-species, *Homo sapiens neanderthalensis*.

Their remains were first discovered in 1856 in the Neander Valley, in Germany. At the time all manner of explanations were put forward – that they were a deformed hermit's bones, or even the remains of someone buried in Noah's flood! But when a nearly complete Neanderthal-type skeleton was uncovered in South-West France in 1908 it caught the world's imagination. The skeleton was reconstructed as a bent, shuffling brute who looked stupid – and who was therefore thought to be stupid.

As more remains came to light the early ideas had to be revised. In 1957 the first skeleton was re-studied. The experts found that this particular Neanderthal Man, who died aged about 40, had suffered from terrible arthritis, and this was what made him bent. The popular picture of Neanderthals had to be changed.

Fossil clues now lead us to believe that Neanderthals were somewhat shorter than we are, but they were also

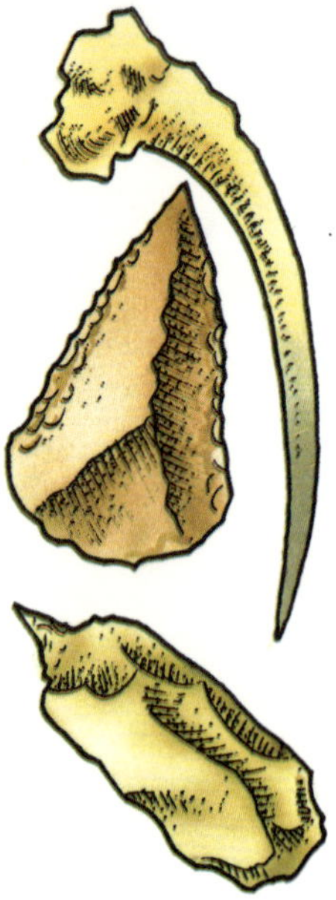

Fine tools
Neanderthal people made fine tools of a type known as Mousterian. There were small and delicate knives, hammer pebbles, scrapers and many other types. With these they hunted woolly rhinoceros, reindeer, hyaena, cave bear, wolf and wild horse.

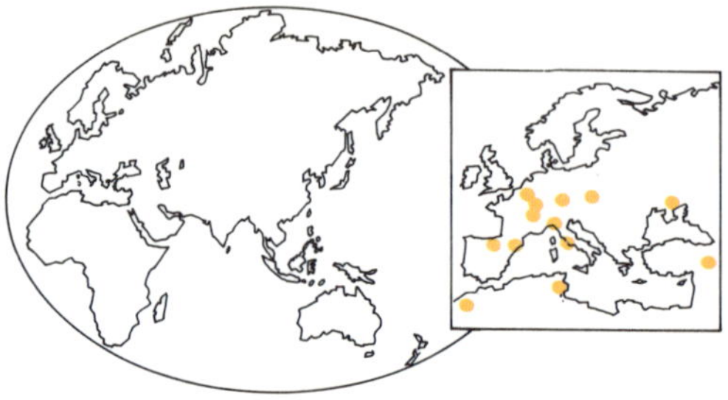

■ = Places where fossils or signs of *Homo sapiens neanderthalensis* have been found.

much stronger, with powerful muscles and joints, and thick bones. They walked upright, like us. Far from being dim-witted because of the supposed 'small brain', measurements show that the average Neanderthaler had a brain slightly larger than that of modern man's. But he did have a flat, sloping forehead and ridges at the eyebrows that made a rather old-fashioned face.

The skeleton of the arthritic man gave other clues. He was badly crippled and his teeth were so bad he could scarcely have chewed. At the time, during the Ice Age, life would have been tough indeed. How did he make it on his own in such a state? Could it be that Neanderthals looked after each other and cared for their sick? We now know that these people buried their dead. Some graves have wild flowers strewn on them. In others the dead people were painted with reddish earth. Perhaps the Neanderthals believed in life after death.

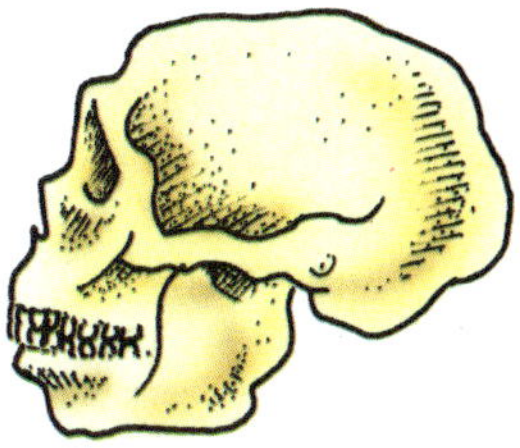

Savage's skull?
The skull of Neanderthal Man, showing the sloping forehead and heavy brow ridges that, at first, made us think of them as stupid and savage.

What happened to the Neanderthals?
The Neanderthal people lived up to 40,000 years ago, during the Ice Age in Europe. Then, quite quickly, they died out. Why? They could have been affected by the climate as the world warmed up again. Or perhaps the waves of modern men migrating across the world killed them off. Then again, it could be that modern people mixed with the Neanderthals and 'absorbed' them by interbreeding.

Fossils of the future

Mankind has come a long way since the first 'ape-men' walked in Africa severa million years ago. But we are a very new species on the Earth. Compared to the length of time that dinosaurs ruled the land, or amphibians dominated the swamps, our time so far in the worlc has passed like the blinking of an eye

Homo sapiens has spread over virtually the whole Earth. We are changing our surroundings at an ever-increasing rate, and very few areas are now truly 'natural'.

The name we have given ourselves *Homo sapiens*, means 'Wise Man' Hopefully it will be more true in the future than it has been in the past, and we will have enough wisdom to menc our ways. If we can avoid nuclear wars, replace some of our natural plan and animal life, and clean up our oceans, we may be able to avoid disaster. If so, what will the fossils of the future look like?

Some evolutionary trends may continue. Physical strength and ability is becoming less important all the time so our bodies may become weaker and less robust. With less chewing to do our teeth, jaws and jaw muscles may become smaller or fewer.

But our physical evolution is slow Compared to it, our mental evolution is racing away. In only a few years we have developed computers that car 'out-think' many a human being. Much of our recent past has centred on changes in our thoughts, outlooks and ideas. Perhaps we are entering a new era, when evolution of the body is taken over by evolution of the mind.

INDEX

A

B

C

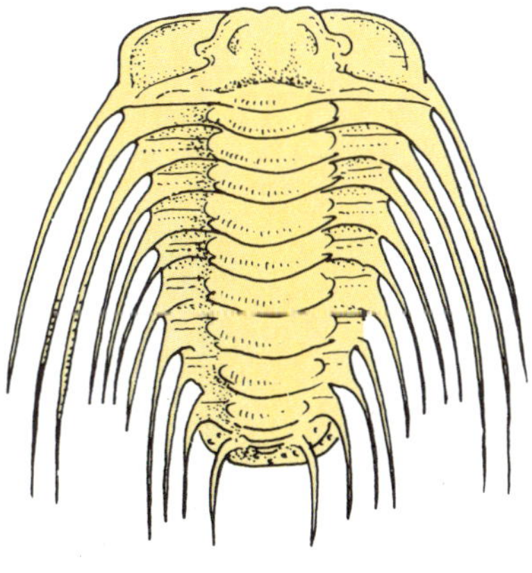

D

E

N

O

P

Q